HOW TO SELL YOUR PHOTOGRAPHS AND ILLUSTRATIONS

Elliott and Barbara Gordon

ALLWORTH PRESS, NEW YORK

Published by Allworth Press, an imprint of Allworth Communications, Inc., 10 East 23rd Street, New York, NY 10010.

Distributor to the trade in the United States and Canada: Writer's Digest Books, an imprint of F&W Publications, Inc., 1507 Dana Avenue, Cincinnati, OH 45207. To order additional copies of this book, call toll-free 1-800-289-0963.

Cover and Book Design by Douglas Design Associates, New York.

Library of Congress Catalog Card Number: 89-085377

ISBN: 0-927629-05-4

DEDICATION

This book is dedicated to all of the creative and talented people everywhere who have a dream of succeeding and the determination to make it a reality.

ACKNOWLEDGMENTS

Our very special thanks to our publisher, Tad Crawford, for his guidance, patience, and faith in us; to Dick Coyne, the publisher of *Communication Arts Magazine*, for his interest; to Kiram Desai of the accounting firm Newley Associates; to SPAR, the Society of Photographers and Artists Representatives, for sharing information with us; to the commercial illustrators and photographers whom we represent, for their confidence in us; to our two boys, Cameron and Tony, for their understanding; and, finally, to all our wonderful clients.

Table of Contents

GETTING YOUR ACT TOGETHER **9**

CHAPTER 1: THE PHOTOGRAPHY AND ILLUSTRATION MARKETS: WHERE THEY ARE AND HOW TO REACH THEM **11**

The Advertising Market 11
- National Consumer Agencies 11
- Industrial Advertising Agencies 12
- Local Advertising Agencies 12
- Pharmaceutical Agencies 12
- Promotion and Direct Response Agencies 13
- A Word About Locations of Advertising Agencies 13
- So Who Does the Buying In These Advertising Agencies? 14

The Publishing Market 14
- General Trade Publishing 14
- The Paperback Market 15
- Special Interest Books 16

The Magazine Market 16

The Corporate Market 17

Other Special Markets of Interest 18
- The Record Album, Cassette, and CD Market 18
- Sales Promotion Agencies 18
- Public Relations Firms 19
- The Art Studio 19
- The Design Studio 19
- Audio/Visual Firms 19
- Newspapers 20
- The Movie Market 20
- Television Networks 21
- The Broadway Theater 21

The Fashion Market 22
- Department Store Advertising 22
- Fashion Advertising Agencies 23
- Fashion Magazines 23
- Retail Catalog Agencies 23

Some Other Special Markets of Interest 24
- The TV Storyboard Market 24
- A Word about the Computer Graphics Market 24
- The Stock Photography Market 24
- The Poster and Calendar Market 25

CHAPTER 2: HOW TO SET UP THE SELLING PORTFOLIO **27**

The Structure of the Portfolio 27
Some General Portfolio Guidelines 28
- The Physical Presentation of the Portfolio 28
- How Many Samples Should be in Your Portfolio 30

Subject Matter —What to Include in the Selling Portfolio 30
The Photographer's Portfolio 34
- The Still-Life Photographer 34
- The People Photographer and the Fashion Photographer 35
- The Beauty Market Photographer 36
- The Annual Report Photographer 37

Illustration: Portfolio Examples 39
Photography: Portfolio Examples 51

CHAPTER 3: PROMOTING AND SELLING THE ARTIST AND PHOTOGRAPHER: THE VALUE OF PROMOTION **57**

Magazine Trade Advertising 58
Direct Mail 59
Directories 59
Mailing Lists 60
- Some Quick Questions and Answers about Mailing Lists 62

Promotion Mailers 63
- Fold-Out 63
- Posters 64
- Oversized Mailers 64
- Small Black and White Promotion Pieces 64
- The Free Promotion Piece 65
- The Best "Freebie" of Them All...Publicity 65
- Some General Promotion Piece Design and Production Tips 66

The Personal Call. 65
Other Promotional Activities 69
Sample Promotional Pieces 70

CHAPTER 4: PRICING — THE FINE ART OF NEGOTIATION **75**

The Ten Key Pricing Questions 76
Market Price Ranges 79
- Magazines 80
- General Trade Books 81
- Paperbacks 81
- Movie Art and Photography Prices 82
- Annual Report Pricing 84

Some Other Important Pricing Areas 84
- "Kill" Fees 84
- Changes 84
- Photography Reshoots 85
- The Purchase Order 85

Some Other Key Questions About Pricing 86
A Word About Copyright and Reproduction Rights 86
Work for Hire 87
Summary 87

CHAPTER 5: MINDING YOUR BUSINESS: SOME IMPORTANT BUSINESS ASPECTS OF COMMERCIAL ART AND PHOTOGRAPHY THAT YOU SHOULD KNOW **89**

The Corporation 89
- The Sub-Chapter "S" Corporation 90

Partnerships and Sole Proprietorships 90
Key Business Considerations 91
- How Much Overhead Do You Need? 91
- What about Record Keeping? 91
- Do You Need Office Help? 91
- What about Billing and Collecting? 92

Business Checklist 94

CHAPTER 6: THE ARTIST AND PHOTOGRAPHER REPRESENTATIVE **95**

Finding and Interviewing an Agent 96
What Does an Agent Do? 96
How Is the Agent Compensated? 97
Billing and Payment Procedures 98
What About Expenses? 98
Who Doesn't Need an Agent? 99
The Importance of the Agent/Talent Contract 100
Key Questions to Ask Agents 101

CHAPTER 7: OPPORTUNITIES FOR THE FREE-LANCE, OUT-OF-TOWN ARTIST AND PHOTOGRAPHER **103**

Realities of Big City Markets for the Out-of-Town Free-Lancer 105
Working Without an Agent 107
Practical Tips for Servicing the Market 107
Now A Word about Expense 109

CHAPTER 8: HOW LONG DOES IT TAKE TO SUCCEED? **111**

ADDENDUM **113**

Professional Organizations and Associations 113
Directories 115
Magazines 117
Forms for Free-Lancers 118

INDEX **123**

ABOUT THE AUTHORS **127**

Getting Your Act Together

The "free-lance" business is one of today's true growth industries. A combination of individuals desiring to be in business for themselves and the business community's desire to save money on taxes and benefit programs by hiring "free-lancers" instead of adding people to the payroll, ensures that this trend will accelerate for the foreseeable future.

It was out of an awareness of this trend and a desire to answer the questions, "Can I make a living as a free-lancer?" asked by students, or, "How can I increase my share of the market?" asked by practicing professionals, that this book was written.

We hope this book will help you to evaluate your talent and potential realistically. We also hope that we will answer many of your practical questions concerning how to get your portfolio into selling shape, how to promote and sell to the many markets, how to price jobs, what form your business should take, whether you should have an agent, and much, much more.

This book was written for both the beginner, who must determine if he or she is ready for the "big plunge," and for the professional, who may have reached market saturation and must contemplate other directions.

Obviously, every potential free-lancer must be aware of certain realities.

First, you must have an overwhelming desire to be in business for yourself. You need to know what the market is buying and how much of a market exists for your talent. This knowledge is acquired through a combination of research, professional consultation, and, in cases where the answer is disappointing, should lead to a redirecting and restructuring of your portfolio.

You must have some knowledge of your area of business. This is usually acquired through a combination of education and work experience.

You will need guidance from a lawyer, an accountant, and a marketing person, plus some kind of banking connection, just as any independent businessman would need.

Because it is difficult to set up any kind of immediate, smooth "cash flow," you will need the resources to stay in business for at least a year, whether this is from your own money in the bank, an investor, a working partner, or your family.

Whether you are a beginner or a working professional who is about to expand his or her markets, your business commandments must always be: Keep The Overhead Low And Don't Overextend Yourself!

Be consistent in your work: you are only as good as your last job. Never stop growing in your craft. Know enough about your business so that you can discuss business situations intelligently with your accountant, banker, lawyer, and others. Keep abreast of market trends and conditions and adapt your talent accordingly. Diversify your market and try not to be a one-client business. Be honest about your work, even if it hurts. Never take anything for granted and if you ever stop enjoying what you are doing, leave the field.

Obviously, we have based much of the information in this book on our own personal experiences as successful agents for commercial illustrators and photographers. However, the book is also the result of extensive research conducted among art directors in all phases of the business, advertising managers, corporate executives, magazine publishers, copyright attorneys, and successful illustrators and photographers.

To all of you, we say: Free-lancing may not be easy emotionally, but you will never be bored, because you never know what is around the next job-prospect corner, and that is one of the excitements of this truly wonderful business.

The Photography and Illustration Markets

1

Where They Are and How to Reach Them

Finding a buyer for your art and photography, regardless of where you live or your style is the key to success in the free-lance business.

This section will talk about the many different markets, where they are, what they buy, and who does the buying.

THE ADVERTISING MARKET

Everyone wants to be in advertising. Ask why and nine out of ten illustrators or photographers will tell you: "It's the money." Sure, they all will say: "I know advertising is very competitive. I know you don't have creative freedom. Sure, I know there is always someone looking over your shoulder every time you press the button on the camera or make a brush stroke. But where else can you potentially make a million dollars, give or take a few hundred thousand?"

And all these illustrators and photographers are right. The advertising business is an insatiable market for art and photography. It literally eats artists up and, just as rudely, tosses them out. But the trip getting to that first million can be exciting.

Most advertising business filters through, and is controlled by, advertising agencies. These agencies can range in size and scope from mega-merger giants like Saachi & Saachi, with billions of dollars in billings, to one- and two-person operations.

By the way, "billings" mean the total amount of advertising dollars placed by an agency in magazines, TV, radio, newspaper, and other media. If an agency "bills" one million dollars, for example, it means that one million dollars was spent by that agency in media on behalf of its clients. The agency traditionally derives its income by taking 15 percent off the top of these billings. In other words, an agency that bills one million dollars generates one hundred and fifty thousand dollars, or 15 percent, in gross income.

But no matter what the size, every advertising agency is a prospect for your illustration or photography.

Let's take a closer look at the different kinds of agencies that make up this incredibly challenging market called advertising.

National Consumer Agencies

These advertising agencies deal in nationally advertised products such as toothpaste, cigarettes, liquor, soap, automobiles, etc., all directed to the national consumer. These national agencies are heavy users of television, both on a national and local level, and also dominate most of the advertising space in national magazines such as

Time, Newsweek, Ladies Home Journal, Cosmopolitan, and many others. Although most of the "big dollar" creative work is in television, national advertising agencies do use a tremendous amount of photography of all types — still life, people, and special effects (just take a look at the major soft-drink advertising that uses both still life and people), and a reasonable amount of illustration (more photography than illustration on a day in, day out basis).

Because of the generally higher prices paid compared with other advertising areas and the volume of photography and illustration used, national consumer agencies are a prime target for every artist and photographer regardless of the competition.

Industrial Advertising Agencies

These agencies bill considerably less than the national advertising agencies, but in one sense may be better prospects for the artist or photographer since they use print as their main advertising vehicle. These agencies also use a very wide range of photographic and illustration styles from the "dead-serious" to fun.

In addition to the advertising dollars spent through magazines and newspapers, industrial agencies also produce a considerable amount of collateral promotion for their clients such as displays, mailers, envelope stuffers, etc., all of which need a wide range of illustration and photography.

The fees paid for art and photography by these industrial agencies are generally lower than the national consumer agencies, since the number of readers (or prospects) reached by industrial advertising is much lower than a national audience, and this has an effect on pricing.

Local Advertising Agencies

Almost every city or town has advertising agencies that service all the local businesses and their advertising needs (the local bank, the supermarket, or, in some cases, branch offices of a major corporation), and these agencies are good prospects for the local artist or photographer.

Because much of the advertising placed by these local advertising agencies is newspaper advertising, any artist or photographer should have a portfolio jam-packed with good black and white illustration or photography covering a wide range of subjects. You won't get rich servicing these local agencies, but you can do a reasonable volume of work, and much of it on a *repeat business basis.*

The advertising fees are not going to match the national or even the industrial agencies, but then again, you might end up getting paid with half a steer from the local supermarket in addition to your standard fee. Everything has its fringe benefits.

Pharmaceutical Agencies

These are advertising agencies that specialize in the advertising and promoting of ethical drugs and other medical products to physicians, pharmacists, and other medical specialists. Strict legal as well as medical restrictions are placed upon most medical advertising produced by these agencies, and the artist or photographer working with pharmaceutical agencies may find he is dealing just as closely with the agency staff doctor as with the art director.

Most of the work is in print advertising although an occasional filmstrip or educational brochure is possible. In addition, doctor detail sheets which spell out what a particular drug can or cannot do represent a very large volume of the work produced by these agencies.

Pharmaceutical agencies use a great variety of illustration styles depending upon the "mood" they are trying to convey, and a tremendous amount of both still-life and people photography. The one restricted area is the medical/ technical area where only a medical illustrator — an artist who has attended medical as well as art school — is used because of his special expertise.

Promotion and Direct Response Agencies

A growing phenomenon in the agency business is the rise of very specialized agencies providing either special forms of promotion or additional services to a client. For example, direct response agencies — agencies that promote your favorite record club or credit card direct to you, the ultimate consumer, are tremendous users of illustration and photography, because their number one medium is print. These agencies may not get the publicity of a network TV buying advertising agency, but they generate a lot of dollars, for themselves, the clients, and you, their friendly free-lancer. Make sure all of them are on your key prospect list.

Also, don't overlook the fact that many large agencies have jumped into the sales promotion business in a big way. Certainly there are independent agencies that specialize in sales promotion, in-store merchandising, and collateral material (more on this later). But the large agencies also are going after this business (as long as they are advertising a product for a client nationally, why not promote that same product on the local level as well and keep more of the "money pie" in-house). This may not seem like very glamorous work to the average photographer or illustrator, with one eye out for a cover of *Time* magazine, but steady work in this area can pay the rent and then some.

A Word About the Location of Advertising Agencies

Although most of the major national advertising agencies have their headquarters in either New York or Chicago, other cities such as Boston, Atlanta, Houston, Dallas, Minneapolis, Los Angeles, and San Francisco are excellent advertising markets. The illustrator or photographer living outside New York or Chicago can sell his services to major agencies, often in the city where he lives, and at the same time get the national recognition and big money that every talent craves.

Also, many national agencies headquartered in New York maintain large branch offices in other cities — branch offices that, in many cases, generate almost as much billing as the home office. These branch offices usually operate fairly autonomously and can make their own buying decisions. Consequently, they are more apt to use good local talent than New York or Chicago talent. Make sure that these branch offices are on your prospect list.

Plus, be on the lookout for markets that are just on the verge of an advertising explosion because of an incredible growth in population. Florida and Arizona are perfect examples of areas that years ago were "advertising graveyards," but now are spending big national as well as local advertising dollars. All are great opportunities for your photography or illustration, and the living isn't too bad, either.

So Who Does The Buying In These Advertising Agencies?

The key person in all of these agencies is the art director, although in large agencies the art buyer, or art buying department is also important. Generally, the art buyer is a person who calls in the free-lance photographer's or illustrator's portfolio to the agency, so that the art director can determine whether that artist is appropriate for the job. The art buyer also solicits job bids from all of the free-lancers — and ultimately issues the purchase orders so they can proceed with the jobs. But the final decision as to who does the job, based on style, reputation, and expertise, is the art director's. Both should be on your promotion list because often both must be sold.

This art director can be very difficult to see. When you do see him, make sure he is a true prospect. Often, art directors are moved around from account to account (this is particularly true of the large national agencies), so an art director who was doing all the print advertising last month and was a great prospect for your art or photography, is now shooting nothing but television commercials and doesn't need you.

Also, since most art directors do not have the time to sit down and talk with every artist or photographer who calls, you must continually promote your services to them. How to do this effectively will be covered in detail in the promotion section of this book, but the importance of promotion cannot be overemphasized. Promote. Promote. Promote. And eventually, the art director will buy, buy, buy.

To summarize: The total advertising market, be it a large national agency, an industrial agency, a local advertising agency, or a special pharmaceutical agency, represents a major market for the commercial illustrator or photographer. Although highly competitive, it is by far the most lucrative of all markets today.

THE PUBLISHING MARKET

Another very large market for the commercial artist or photographer is the book market. There are three distinct and separate areas of book publishing and these will be covered in this section.

General Trade Publishing

This market can cover everything from children's books to hard-cover best sellers to textbooks, all sold through established stores or book-store chains. This business is generated through the major publishing houses, such as Macmillan, Simon & Schuster, Random House, and others.

These publishing houses use a large amount of illustration of all styles (photorealism, stylized realism, fun, etc., in both color and black and white), and a smaller amount of photography. Often, these publishing houses will buy "art packages" from recognized artist representatives specializing in the book field. A publisher, for example, might commit a certain number of books to these "packagers" for a specified price covering the entire project including, in some cases, type and mechanicals as well as artwork. If you are represented by these large book agents, then you have an excellent chance to work on a variety of projects and make a reasonable amount of money.

However, as an individual artist or photographer, you can also approach publishers directly. If your style is right for a particular book, you may get the chance to illustrate that book.

Although prices are generally lower than in other markets, particularly for the amount of work you do, deadlines are usually quite reasonable, working conditions can be very pleasant, and you can end up doing some lovely things, which you will be proud to carry in your portfolio.

Obviously, art styles will vary considerably, from delicate, children's-book-type illustration, to hard-edged technical illustration for manuals or textbooks. However, this general trade publishing field, including publishers catering to the reading consumer and those appealing strictly to the vast educational market, can offer good opportunities to both the beginner and the "working" illustrator. The field's demand for all kinds of art is almost insatiable.

These publishers also use photography, but not nearly as often as illustration. Thus, this market does not represent a major opportunity for the free-lance photographer. Photography fees are quite low compared to advertising and other areas, so it may be difficult for the free-lance photographer to make a good living in this market.

One final word about this market. If you can write and illustrate your own book, then you can usually make more money, thanks to the royalties, than you can if you illustrate someone else's book. Even so, this is a very tough and demanding market and a difficult way for most illustrators to make a living.

The Paperback Market

Without a doubt, paperbacks are the wave of the present, as well as the future, in the book publishing field, and represent an excellent opportunity for both the illustrator and the photographer.

The paperback market is centered in New York City, and the art director of the paperback company does the buying of art and photography.

What kind of illustration style do these paperback houses buy? Well, walk into any drugstore, supermarket, airport waiting lounge, or even a bookstore and take a look at the range of titles produced by these houses. Historical and modern romance. Westerns. Science fiction. The subjects are limitless. And yet the art style, in 99 percent of the cases, is photorealism. Why? Because every paperback house has research on file that says quite simply: "Put the plot on the cover in a real style the customer can understand at a glance. Don't get cute. Just tell the reader what the book is about in two seconds or less." That doesn't mean a special book on poetry might not use a "soft" or stylized type of illustration, but these kinds of books are few and far between. Unless you do photorealism, the paperback market might not be for you.

Photography — and there is a reasonable amount bought by the paperback houses — is also hard-sell. You are not doing pretty pictures. Just ones that sell books. Fees, for both illustration and photography, are reasonable and sometimes exceptional, depending upon the reputation and skill of the artist or photographer.

To sum up: Whoever said you can't tell a book by its cover never sold a paperback. If you understand the philosophy and have the art or photography style to match, you can make a very comfortable and steady living in the mass-market paperback business.

Special Interest Books

Another book area exists that commercial illustrators and photographers should exploit. Special interest publishers, such as Time-Life Books, Readers Digest, Franklin Library, and others, publish special historical books, "how-to" books, one-of-a-kind collectible books, commemorative books, and books and novels of special interest to readers throughout the country. (The Readers' Digest Condensed Novels are examples of this type.) Lead time in this market is good, prices are quite competitive, and often the illustrator or photographer has a great deal of creative freedom.

Many of these companies also have special merchandising divisions that produce record albums, commemorative plates, etc. — all of which use art and photography. Many an illustrator or photographer has carved out a very rewarding and secure living from these special interest publishers. Do not overlook them.

An important note about the overall publishing business today. Mergers between major publishing houses have become almost commonplace, so that the concentration of book publishing is centered in large publishing conglomerates. What these mergers mean is that there is much more emphasis on the fiction and non-fiction "blockbuster," and little room left for the midlist book, the moderate money-maker that provides the largest market for most illustrators and photographers. Merger-mania not only is a fact of life in the advertising business, but has become common in the once sedate and predictable publishing business.

THE MAGAZINE MARKET

A very fertile market for both illustrators and photographers is the magazine market. All of the major consumer magazines—*McCall's*, *Time*, *Newsweek*, *Sports Illustrated*, *TV Guide*, plus business magazines such as *Fortune*, *Forbes*, and *Business Week*—buy large amounts of art and photography. Each magazine has an art director in charge of purchasing art and photography.

It is common practice now for the illustrator or photographer to drop the portfolio off, often on pre-designated days, so the art director can evaluate the work. It is almost impossible to see these magazine art directors personally. Don't despair: The art director will look, often along with his editors.

One word of caution. Before you drop your portfolio off, buy a copy of the magazine you are interested in, read it, and see what kind of illustration or photography the magazine is using. Don't waste your time or the art director's time if what you are doing is completely inappropriate to what the magazine is buying (you are into soft sculpture and the magazine is into realistic portraits). You can do yourself a great deal of harm if you fail to research your market.

The prices paid for illustration and photography in these national or major magazines are fairly high. Each magazine has a page rate (more on this later in the pricing section of this book), and the illustrator will be called upon to illustrate a particular story or article on assignment from the art director. Magazines use a variety of art within their formats, depending upon the "mood" of the story to be captured. If you are unable to get an assignment illustrating a cover or major piece in the magazine, you might be assigned the task of illustrating small "spots" which accompany special columns or features. These "spots" may use a variety of styles.

Although the fees may not be as high as national advertising fees, these magazines can give the illustrator national recognition. No wonder the competition can get hectic!

Women's magazines use a fair amount of photography, both on the food and home economic pages. Photojournalism and portrait work is used extensively in the business and news magazine area. Again, read the magazines to see what kind of photography they are buying. If your style is consistent with what they are publishing, go after them.

Special Interest Magazines

The number of general magazines has declined in the past ten years because of the growth of television. In their place, an entirely new kind of magazine has emerged and grown dramatically. These magazines, called special interest magazines, cater to a specialized consumer who is interested in one particular subject.

They are excellent markets for both illustration and photography and use a full range of styles depending upon the article to be illustrated or the subject to be shot. Although fees are not as high as the national magazines, and the recognition factor may not be as great, don't overlook special interest magazines for a steady source of income and satisfaction.

Some local city and town newspapers have special Sunday supplements that buy art and photography. You might not get rich servicing these local supplements, but they can help you build up your portfolio and give you invaluable experience, as well as making you very well known in your home town. In addition to Sunday supplements, many major cities — perhaps 25 or more — have their own general "city" magazine, or a city business magazine or tabloid.

THE CORPORATE MARKET

Another opportunity is the direct company market. Companies often purchase art and photography direct for annual reports, special company magazines, in-house employee brochures, company newsletters, etc. For example, many companies publish excellent in-house magazines that go to all of their stockholders and other influential people. Quality-wise, they are equal to almost any magazine published today.

Most in-house magazines have a staff art director responsible for buying art and photography. Fees can be quite competitive, and illustration styles can vary depending upon editorial subjects.

Every major corporation must publish an annual report. This is an excellent opportunity for the photographer whose portfolio is geared to this market (good people pictures and industrial shots are a must). The fees are good, the recognition factor can be excellent, and one can almost make a living doing just annual reports for companies throughout the country.

Although annual reports are often produced by outside agencies such as public relations firms or others specializing in this work, the ultimate annual report decision rests with the corporation's public relations office, so you should make people in this department aware of your talents. At the very minimum, a good mailing piece or a letter enclosing a mailing piece should be sent to corporate public relations departments if a personal call is not feasible.

The corporate advertising department should also be on your list of prospects because these departments are often responsible for a tremendous amount of collateral promotional material and are good prospects for virtually all kinds of art and photography.

Working directly for corporations, either on an annual report, a company brochure, or a display can mean repeat business at a profit. Corporations often turn into lasting and satisfied customers.

OTHER SPECIAL MARKETS OF INTEREST

In addition to the major markets mentioned previously, there are special markets that can represent an excellent source of work for both the illustrator and photographer.

The Record Album, Cassette and CD Market

Every young illustrator or photographer wants to crack the record album cover market. It is often the closest he will come to being part of the entertainment business. Record companies such as RCA, Polygram, Arista, CBS, and others, located in New York and Los Angeles, are usually receptive to new art and photography looks and will often take a chance on a new and unproven talent. Artistically, whether you are a beginner or a veteran, record album covers give you the chance, more often than not, to "do your own thing," and you will probably end up with a good sample for your portfolio.

However, fees paid are lower than those paid in other markets, except when a record album cover is done for a nationally known group and a nationally known artist is commissioned to do the job. But, if an album cover job comes along, take it.

Sales Promotion Agencies

These agencies can be independent companies doing sales promotion projects for a variety of clients, including advertising agencies, or can be a separate department or division of an advertising agency, public relations firm, or company. Most of the work done by these firms consists of brochures, mailers, displays, posters, etc., and almost any kind of art style is used depending upon what is needed for a specific project. Some photography is used, the type of photography (still-life, people, etc.) also dictated by the project.

You will probably not receive much recognition from your peers or a national audience for work done in the sales promotion area, but what you lose in personal recognition, you can make up in sheer volume...volume that can add up to very significant dollars.

Public Relations Firms

These companies often maintain their own independent art staffs headed by an art director, but do buy free-lance art and photography. If you are an annual report photographer, this is the kind of agency you should be calling on. These agencies are also excellent markets for straightforward, realistic illustration. Many of these large public relations firms are competing with advertising agencies in the range of services being offered, including national print and television advertising campaigns, so they should be high on your prospect list.

The Art Studio

Because of past economic conditions and changes in the ways of doing business, the large art studio in most metropolitan areas is almost a thing of the past. Prices paid per job on work handled through studios are consistently lower than in other areas because the studio must put its own mark-up on the cost of art and photography before submitting a bill to the client. Consequently, the studios pay lower prices for art and photography in order to insure themselves a reasonable profit. That fact, combined with the small number of art studios left in the field, reduces their importance as possible job prospects for the artist or photographer.

The Design Studio

These studios work directly for companies and handle a great number of challenging illustration and photographic projects. Again, because the studio must mark up all services, art and photography prices will normally be lower than those paid by advertising agencies or companies.

The essential difference between a design studio and an art studio is the way artists, in particular, are contracted for work. Design studios generally use free-lance artists and photographers and maintain only designers on staff.

Art studios, on the other hand, not only maintain a group of artists, either on staff or free-lance, but also act as the selling agent for the artist. At one time, the art studio served as an excellent training ground for the new artist entering the field, but that opportunity, unfortunately, no longer exists.

The design studio represents a much better prospect for free-lance art and photography, although the small art studio in your home town might also be a prospect.

Audio/Visual Firms

By establishing a good working relationship with an audio/visual firm, one that provides slides for annual company meetings, special sales conferences, etc., on a continual basis, a photographer can earn a good, steady income. Although many of the major firms are located in New York and Los Angeles, opportunities for the audio/visual photographer exist in almost any city in the country.

Newspapers

Newspaper advertisements are normally prepared by advertising agencies, and, if you have a strong black and white illustration or photography book, this could be the market for you. Most newspaper art and photography is used for food and soft-drink clients, with the emphasis on the coupon advertisement ("clip the coupon and get a free box of cereal"). The art and photography is very hard-sell and realistic and must be suitable for excellent newspaper reproduction. Fortunes have been made by those few illustrators who specialize in hard-sell black and white food or product illustration, even though most people in the art community might not even recognize their names.

This black and white newspaper advertising is handled by the art director at the advertising agency assigned to specific food or other accounts. He may buy both black and white and color illustrations or photography, depending upon the needs of his client at that particular moment. Similarly, the art director on a corporate account might use good black and white illustration in a general newspaper campaign (executives in meetings or on a business trip, or an industrial vignette) geared for *The Wall Street Journal* or other major newspapers, and so will be looking for illustrators or photographers with good, strong, black and white portfolio pieces.

In addition to newspaper advertising handled through advertising agencies, your local newspaper editorial department also buys art and photography. Art styles can range from the esoteric to a fairly realistic style. Fees are low (the "life" of an illustration is no more than twenty-four hours), and speed is an absolute essential. If the newspaper does not have an artist on staff (and some do), working for your local newspaper on a regular free-lance basis can generate some good income.

The newspaper art director is the one to see. In the big city dailies, that may mean seeing a number of different art directors, each one responsible for a particular section of the newspaper.

The Movie Market

Everyone wants to work for the movies. It is glamorous. It is exciting. And it can create ulcers. But you can be paid quite handsomely for those ulcers.

Most movie art is purchased through movie advertising agencies or "boutiques," or, more specifically, companies that are either independently owned or are a separate division of a major advertising agency that specializes in movie advertising. In addition, film studios may commission movie art themselves, so if you live in California, be sure to investigate them.

Although an occasional "fun" or decorative illustration might sneak through, most of the movie art used is photorealistic.

It has been said that the life of a movie advertising campaign is three days — you either get the customers in the door then, or the movie "dies." The movie poster or movie advertisement must tell the plot line and tell it fast. Movie art can be used for full-color poster art or for black and white newspaper advertising (often the same piece of art), and the artist is paid according to usage.

The movie industry is also an excellent prospect for the photographer — both still-life and people — but again, the emphasis is on "over-kill," namely, the hard-sell approach.

In most cases, well-known movie stars have first approval on all art produced, so you had better be good at likenesses. Also, make sure you cover up all the wrinkles no matter how old the star may be.

The fees paid for both art and photography accepted for use in the final movie poster or advertising campaign can be quite staggering, particularly for big budget movies. (Stories abound in the industry concerning money made by big talents who not only sent their kids through college but ended up buying the college as well.)

On the other hand, someone has to do the "B" movie art, and the fees might be just barely enough to pay last month's overdue rent. (The complexity of movie pricing will be fully discussed in the pricing section).

Competition is intense ("incredible" might be a better word) with movie agencies commissioning ten or even twenty artists to work on the same movie poster, winner take all. However, if you win, you will probably get more work in the movie area — and find yourself not only enjoying the excitement of the business, but the national prestige and recognition as well. Especially if the last movie you worked on was a "blockbuster."

Television Networks

In the past, when someone mentioned network TV, one automatically thought of the big three: NBC, CBS, and ABC. Now one has to add the Ted Turners, the Rupert Murdochs, HBO, and other cable TV networks that are pulling big advertising dollars away from the three networks. All produce both internal and external advertisements and collateral material and all are ideal markets for both illustrators and photographers.

New York is the main source of network television art, and most of that is bought through the network art department staffed with a number of art directors, each handling a particular area of network TV advertising or promotion. However, your local television station also needs art and could be a good prospect for your work.

In addition to network black and white newspaper advertising, a tremendous amount of promotional material — both in color and black and white — is produced in these network art departments for local network affiliates throughout the country.

Art styles range from the caricature of the latest network "phenom" to superrealistic "movie-type" art, so almost any style of illustration has a shot at this market. Keep those good color and black and white portraits handy and at the top of your portfolio.

The Broadway Theater

Basically, this market is unique to New York, although local theater groups in your area might commission you to do a show poster on occasion. Because Broadway shows often have a very limited life span, the budgets for most Broadway posters are small compared to the movies, even though the amount of work may be exactly the same. If the show is a success, your artwork may be used for programs, special promotions, etc., and that could mean extra money for you.

When working for Broadway, stay away from the "bombs" — and if you can tell which show will do that in advance, you should either be a show "angel" or a critic. After all, you want your art to get years of exposure.

Photography is also used on Broadway (about equal to the amount of illustration used), but, again, the photographic fees are not as high as in the movie industry.

Broadway, interestingly, offers more flexibility in the kind of art styles used with a much greater emphasis on "design-y" illustration and not so much on realism.

THE FASHION MARKET

The fashion market, situated primarily in New York but truly world-wide in scope and impact, is probably the most competitive market in the business today. The market can be broken down into the following different areas:

Department Store Advertising

Fashion illustration and photography is most visible in department store advertisements — the Macy's, Bergdorf-Goodmans, Bloomingdale's, Nieman-Marcuses, and many more. All of these stores purchase large amounts of both fashion art and photography, not only for the daily advertisements they run, but also for merchandise catalogs produced in-house.

Getting work from these department stores on a regular basis may be very difficult for either the illustrator or photographer. Frequently, department stores will sign a well-known illustrator or a new illustrator with a distinctive style to a long-term contract — up to a year or more — committing that illustrator to produce up to five advertisements a week for that department store on an exclusive basis. Contracts may be signed with photographers as well. Those illustrators and photographers under contract are guaranteed an income for the life of the contract in return for producing a tremendous amount of work.

Most of the illustration and photography is black and white since the ads will be running in newspapers. However, color photography is used when in-house merchandise catalogs are shot. Obviously, there is a "style" to any fashion illustration or fashion photograph and both the artist and photographer must create a "fashion" look, via attractive models and a real flair for the clothes, with the proper drama and accent used in the photograph (through lighting) or the illustration. You should be specially trained in the fashion area if that is where you want to earn your living. Very high volume (with small fees paid for each photograph or illustration) is normal in the fashion business and you must be able to handle that. It may be difficult to get into department store advertising, but if you want to be in the fashion area, you must call on the department stores, either in New York or in your local area.

Fashion Advertising Agencies

These are advertising agencies which specialize in the advertising of clothes, accessories, and other fashion specialties. These agencies produce national and trade advertising — in color and black and white — for both magazines and newspapers. (Television advertising is also used if the product has a large enough budget.)

These agencies are closely allied to the "garment" business and are used to tight deadlines, hard-sell approaches and limited advertising fees. The fashion agency is a "natural" for the fashion photographer or the fashion illustrator. The conventional illustrator or photographer might have an occasion to work for fashion agencies like these if a non-fashion look is sought for variation.

Fashion Magazines

Everyone is familiar with the well-known fashion magazines, such as *Vogue*, *Harper's Bazaar*, *Mademoiselle*, and *Glamour*, which lead the way when it comes to showcasing fashion photography and illustration. Anyone who gets the opportunity to work for any of them should take it. There have been many fashion photographers and illustrators whose reputations have been made by a spread or series of pages in one of these prestigious magazines.

Retail Catalog Agencies

There are many agencies which specialize in producing merchandise catalogs for department stores and special clothing manufacturers. These catalogs show page after page of saleable merchandise and are produced, in most cases, by still-life and people or fashion photographers. The intent of the catalog is to sell merchandise, so these catalogs do not normally offer the most creative opportunities for the photographer. Recently, however, there has been a trend toward catalogs with greater flair, especially among department stores that focus on fashion.

As a photographer, you must shoot fast and turn out volume. In other words, you must be set up for business with good, available studio space (even if you rent it for the occasion) and several good assistants.

Catalogs are usually offered on a "package price" basis (the catalog agency has to put their mark-up on everything). The photographer must shoot a lot of film for not a great deal of money. Nonetheless, these catalogs have kept a great number of photographers in business.

The catalog market for illustrators is much more limited because catalogs are basically "hard-sell" vehicles and photography is a much better medium for the "hard-sell" approach. Occasionally, however, a catalog will combine both, so catalog agencies should not be overlooked as a source of income for illustrators.

In all cases, the art director is the person to see — at the department store, the fashion magazine, the retail catalog agency, or the fashion advertising agency. These art directors know the fashion and merchandising business and know the kind of illustration and photography that is right for each project. Although these art directors may occasionally use a "non-fashion" talent, their specific needs will exclude most general illustrators and photographers. If this is your specialty, you will find the fashion market the most exciting, challenging, and possibly the most lucrative area in the entire free-lance territory.

SOME OTHER SPECIAL MARKETS OF INTEREST

The TV Storyboard Market

Every advertising agency involved in television frequently needs illustrators who can do storyboard work. For the illustrator or photographer just starting out, or possibly changing careers, the ability to create story-boards can provide a speedy entrance into the advertising business.

A storyboard shows a series of vignettes or scenes which will form the basis of a "live" or animated television commercial. The work entails illustrating product, people, or events in a twelve-inch-by-twelve-inch diagonal area — frame by frame — with a total of from twelve to twenty-four frames constituting a typical storyboard.

Artwork is done in color — with paint or magic markers — and the style is quite realistic.

A typical storyboard might show a housewife in the kitchen preparing supper with the client's products and then proceed through the steps she takes to make the product identifiable and attractive. However, any scene or scenes for a television commercial can be produced in a storyboard. These storyboards are used by the agency to obtain client approval for the commercial as well as outlining to the art director and the producer the kind of live or animated action to be shot.

Although agencies often maintain a staff of storyboard artists, many agencies buy storyboards free-lance. The art buyer in major advertising agencies or the personnel manager in smaller agencies should be contacted for storyboard work.

A storyboard can also be shot by a photographer. Fees for both photography and illustration storyboards are priced on a per-frame basis and, although you will never get rich on this work (and certainly will receive little or no recognition except from the art director), storyboards can produce income and give you an inside look at the advertising business.

A Word about the Computer Graphics Market

There is no question that computers are adding another dimension to the world of the free lancer. Computer graphics can not only create new and interesting effects (as well as fully dimensionalized artwork), but can often do it in half the time. No, the computer will never truly replace the artist, but it can and does provide a new avenue of opportunity for any artist who knows how to use one. Storyboards, special presentation art, key animated art, and much more can all be created on the computer and produced on a free-lance basis as well as by staff. Make sure you don't overlook the unlimited opportunities available for the artist who is comfortable in the wonderful world of computer graphics.

The Stock Photography Market

Like the rest of the commercial photography market, the stock photography market has certain requirements. Usually more commercially-oriented photographs do better than esoteric and artistic ones.

Photographs should be on 35mm slides, should be captioned (e.g., A view of San Juan), and the photographer should have all the necessary model releases.

The same clients who buy commercial photography — the advertising agencies, magazines, books, etc. — are potential customers for stock photographs. That is another reason why your stock photography portfolio should be as commercially geared as your regular portfolio.

Some stock agencies will want at least three thousand slides made available to them, and it is not unusual for a photographer who is making an excellent income on his stock shots to have as many as twenty-five thousand slides on file.

The best bet for the photographer considering the stock photography route is to approach several agencies or representatives. The agency can immediately evaluate the photographer's "stock" potential based on the slides available.

A stock photography agency may ask a photographer to sign a five-year contract and take a fifty-percent commission on all sales. But, since stock photographs represent existing shots, they can be an easy way for a photographer to realize extra income on his inventory.

The Poster and Calendar Market

Some poster or calendar art and photography is commissioned directly from the artist while some is commissioned from stock art and photography. (The companies will purchase a specific reproduction right for use as a poster, etc., from a piece of art or photography that the free-lancer owns outright.)

Often the purchaser in both of these markets likes to operate on a royalty basis, which means the free-lancer is paid based on the number of posters or calendars sold. On the surface, this looks and sounds like a fair way to deal, but because royalties are so hard to police, and especially in cases where a free-lancer has put forth time and effort to produce a new piece of work, we strongly recommend that the free-lancer get an advance against royalties. That advance should represent at least 50 percent of the royalties that the work is expected to produce. In this way, the free-lancer has at least some minimum guarantee of payment for his or her work. Ownership of the original work should also be established from the start, and if the publisher wishes to own the original work, additional monies should be paid.

When dealing with a royalty situation, it's always good to have a contract spelling eveything out. Provisions should be made to have an independent auditor available to investigate the sales records and monitor the royalty situation. Our experience has been that, once a work is printed, it is sometimes very difficult to keep track of the sales of the product and therefore the royalties, unless specific monitoring situations are set up for this purpose.

To put it simply, the most important thing to know about selling any market is to KNOW THAT MARKET. Take a good hard look at all the markets and

WHAT THEY ARE BUYING in both illustration and photography. Take a look at what you are doing, both in style and subject matter, to see what markets you are best qualified to sell.

Very few artists or photographers are appropriate for all markets, so go after those markets which represent the highest dollar potential to you. Promote to those markets. Work in those markets. Get repeat business in those markets. Searching out and selling the RIGHT MARKET FOR YOU can be as important as developing the right photographic or illustration style. It is a critical part of any artist's or photographer's career plan.

How to Set Up the Selling Portfolio

The most important thing you will ever do as a professional photographer or illustrator is to set up your selling portfolio. There is a definite "formula" to doing this. As it would in any business, your portfolio represents your inventory and must be kept up to date. This section will spell out the "formula" for keeping your portfolio inventory saleable and ready for market at all times.

If you were going into any other business — a clothing store, management consulting, electronics, etc. — you would first determine what the marketplace was buying and in what quantities. You would then gear your inventory to the marketplace at a realistic price, with ample distribution. Why shouldn't the illustrator or photographer do the same thing? There are certain markets for specific types of art and photography (see the section on markets). There are also, in many instances, certain kinds of illustrations or photographs that are bought in greater quantity than others. Yes, there are always exceptions to the rule, and certain talents do work in one specialty profitably. But the majority of free-lancers work over a wide spectrum of markets. This is what this portfolio section will explore.

THE STRUCTURE OF THE PORTFOLIO

Unfortunately, most illustrators and photographers set up their portfolios haphazardly. Their portfolios include old art or photography, school assignments (certainly this is true if they are beginning free-lancers), jobs they did in the past, regardless of quality, or pieces they happen to like. But if you ask the free-lancer which markets this portfolio is intended for, he usually looks as if you were speaking in a foreign language. And yet, isn't it reasonable to have your presentation pointed toward a specific market or markets? It is far better to have a portfolio that is structured purposefully than one that is put together casually and on the off chance that it might be right for some particular job.

Let's be honest. The selling portfolio doesn't just happen by chance. It is deliberately and carefully engineered.

At one time, when art directors had more jobs to hand out and unlimited freedom, a less structured portfolio could get work for a talent. But in today's tough economic and competitive climate — when there are forty to one hundred possible illustrators or photographers for every job, where the art director or art buyer can call in anywhere from five to fifty portfolios to show the client — one can see that the content of the portfolio is critical. Quite often, a properly structured portfolio will get the free-lancer a job over a better artist, who didn't know the "formula" or didn't try to organize a selling portfolio.

What, then, should go into the general portfolio — the portfolio that is geared to a wide selection of advertising and editorial market opportunities?

Let's start with the portfolio you now have. Chances are, at least some of the things you have among your current samples should not be there. So your first task — and it's a tough one — is to edit brutally.

As you examine each piece in your portfolio ask yourself: "Where is the market for this particular piece?" And be honest. Don't say that this is the type of painting or photography the market should be buying. Instead, ask whether this particular portfolio piece is what the market really is buying.

For example, when your photograph or illustration contains people, are they the kind of people who hold a major credit card? Or go to the country club dance? Or mow their own lawn on Sunday? If the answer is "no," then probably the people in your portfolio are not appropriate for the general advertising or editorial market.

When products are involved, ask yourself whether you have ever seen any kind of advertising for this product. For example, you may love that radish shot of yours, but have you ever seen an advertising campaign for a radish? In other words, the product shot or illustration in your portfolio must be truly market-oriented and identifiable by the average consumer.

Now this doesn't mean that you can't have a non-commercial or experimental piece in your portfolio. But it does mean that you must have a "hard core" of commercial samples as well as those experimental pieces which show off your creative expertise. If you keep the ratio of two-thirds commercial portfolio pieces to one-third experimental pieces, then you'll probably start to find that your selling portfolio will pull in more jobs.

So start with merciless editing, retaining only the best and most commercial work. For example, the tear sheet for that most prestigious client whom you hated because the job really didn't show you to the best advantage has no place in your selling portfolio. In fact, it is better to have one good unpublished piece than to have ten bad or unworthy published pieces. Remember: The art director is looking for the strongest talent possible to do his assignment and you should never put doubts in his mind by showing him anything less than your best work. The process of editing, by the way, will continue throughout your professional career. Editing your current portfolio down to what shows you off to the very best advantage must be done now.

SOME GENERAL PORTFOLIO GUIDELINES

The Physical Presentation of the Portfolio

Since you are dealing, for the most part, with a print medium, and art directors you are calling on are print-oriented art directors, it is usually a good idea to have portfolio samples in a form that is easy for the art director to handle and examine. A carousel of 35mm slides is not as effective as 8-by-10-inch transparencies, laminated tear sheets, or large mounted prints (no larger than 16-by-20 inches). Usually, loose samples are preferred to samples in a ring-binder simply because the art director can take a few prints or transparencies and use them in his presentation to the client without a great deal of trouble. Also, loose samples let you gear your presentation to a specific art director on a specific account — difficult to do when all the samples are in a ring binder.

When dealing with print, the art director likes something he can hold in his hands instead of something he has to view on a screen because the loose samples more closely approximate his actual working medium (the one exception is animatics and photomatics where the 35mm slide carousel actually works to your advantage). Also, every free-lancer should have more than one portfolio. One of these duplicate portfolios should be on 35mm slides for easy air-freighting to out-of-town agencies. Your everyday working portfolio, however, should be on transparencies or prints. For the photographer, this is usually no problem, but for the illustrator, it is always a good idea to get the piece of art photographed before delivering it to the client. Another advantage of transparencies, by the way, is that you can get the new piece into your portfolio immediately. Since tear sheets are a long time in coming and are also often of poor reproduction quality, transparencies make a great deal of sense.

The order of samples presented in a portfolio will depend, of course, upon who the art director is and what specific account he is working on. For example, an art director on a travel account will be more interested in seeing people samples than product samples. The portfolio should be "tailored" and "weighted" for that art director's eyes only. This does not mean that other samples featuring different subjects should be eliminated completely. It simply means that they should take "second billing" to the primary people samples that will grab this particular art director's attention.

Obviously, if you are making a general exploratory call on an art director, and you do not know what account he or she is working on, samples showing a variety of subjects are appropriate. The art director will not only see your complete range of abilities, but may also enjoy looking at the entire portfolio.

As mentioned in other sections of the book, the practice of dropping off the portfolio is widespread today. You should have a duplicate portfolio ready to go. How else can you make that personal call while your portfolio is in Chicago or Atlanta or being evaluated at some magazine? Spend money to duplicate your best portfolio pieces and make up as many portfolios as you think you need.

The portfolio should always be in first-class condition. This includes the portfolio case as well as the samples. Too often, beautiful samples submitted by an illustrator or photographer are minimized by the outward appearance of the carrying case. The portfolio case should be clean and in good working condition (ever try to open a portfolio when the zipper or latch refuses to open? No art director will take the time to call a locksmith. He'll just give the job to someone else).

Your name also should be displayed prominently on the outside of the portfolio — just how flamboyant depends upon your personality, but it is free advertising — and your address and telephone number should be included on both the outside and inside.

In addition, all of the transparencies or printed pieces in your portfolio should bear your name, address, and telephone number. The art director will probably be using these pieces independently of each other and you want to make sure he knows whose samples they are and where to call you with the job. Also, this prevents your samples being misplaced or lost — which does happen.

Finally, you must include in the portfolio at least one "leave-behind" promotion piece, so the art director can keep it on file if there is no immediate job. Do this, even though you have already done a general mailing of that same promotion piece. A "leave-behind" piece will help keep you current in the mind of that art director.

How Many Samples Should Be in Your Portfolio?

There are no hard and fast rules, but your portfolio should have a minimum of ten working pieces — either transparencies, tear sheets, or a combination of both. Don't overload the portfolio with too many samples just because you feel quantity will impress the art director. It really doesn't work that way. An art director can tell by flipping through as few as four or five samples whether you are the right photographer or illustrator for his job. Putting thirty or more diverse pieces in a portfolio will probably turn him off completely. Every art director quivers in his levis when he looks down the hall and sees an artist or photographer moving toward him lugging two complete 35mm carousels containing one hundred and sixty samples, knowing full well that it will take at least an hour of his time. After the interview, the art director won't care to remember it and probably hopes that talent never calls him again.

Ten of your best portfolio pieces will position you in the art director's mind immediately and make it very easy for him to remember you. Of course, if you have just completed three or four absolutely dynamite shots that you must show someone, then by all means, add them to the portfolio. But stay away from the "I'm going to bury you with information until you buy" approach.

SUBJECT MATTER — WHAT TO INCLUDE IN THE SELLING PORTFOLIO

Although every portfolio can vary from call to call depending upon what you think the art director will want to see in relation to his account, every single general portfolio should have certain pieces that not only demonstrate your style but cover all market areas that you are trying to sell. Keep in mind that the most successful illustrators and photographers are those who work in all markets — not just one or two. And it makes sense. When work is slow in one market, you can pick up the slack in another.

So your portfolio should show that you can work in any market — an art director might type-cast your style, but he certainly won't be able to type-cast you when it comes to the markets where you can work.

With that as an objective, the following is a suggested checklist of samples that should be found in the general illustrator's or photographer's portfolio (specific photography samples will be covered in more detail later in this section). These sample subject matters are applicable to both areas.

The Boy/Girl Sample

Picture the typical middle-class boy and girl in their twenties, attractive, but not "model" beautiful, having fun together. Maybe they are married, standing before their house in the suburbs enjoying the "good life." Or possibly the couple in love are having a picnic on the beach or in a field; romance is in the air. Or perhaps the couple is having dinner at one of those intimate French bistros. Where you put them is up to you. But the boy/girl sample will be appropriate for a wide variety of advertising and editorial markets and will play an important part in your portfolio.

The Travel or General Sample

Here is what might be described as the perfect sample. First, it shows beautiful people having fun and a hotel in the background (that shows how you handle architecture). Happy activities such as water-skiing, boating, swimming, etc., are a "must." Perhaps a romantic vignette showing lovers in the hotel restaurant or nightclub can be added. All of these elements are not only perfect for the obvious airline or travel account but for soft drink, liquor, cigarette, or any other "people-oriented" account.

But, perhaps most important, a good, complicated, crammed-full-of-everything general sample shows how you design. It shows how you handle, in a tasteful and interesting way, a variety of different elements in one illustration or photograph.

A good travel sample is a working sample and is ideal for a number of different markets. If you don't have one in your portfolio, it should become a high priority.

The Paperback Romantic Sample

People in the world of paperbacks are different from those found in the cigarette or soft-drink advertisements because paperback people live in a world of pure fantasy. Consequently, the effectiveness of this sample will depend a great deal on your casting of the models. Are men really that virile and women really that beautiful? Of course not. But they sure sell books.

Again, the couple is in love and involved in some romantic situation. For the specialized romance, you might even try an historical romance sample — authentic costuming and all. In any event, a good romantic sample done in the right photorealistic style could get you into the paperback company door.

The Movie and/or Portrait Sample

The movie star is omnipotent. He or she demands strong and flattering likenesses. So the movie star picture reference is critical. But, paradoxically, the movie star alone makes for a boring sample. Juice it up with a montage of key scenes from the star's last few movies or television extravaganzas. By doing that, the art director will see your design ability at work.

However, make sure the movie star you pick — and this is true of any portrait you do for your portfolio — is instantly recognizable and current. Stay away from yesterday's heroes or stars, including athletes. Do not use any politician. Nothing dates a sample more than last year's election. Do a current, well-known "hot" movie star — man or woman, or both — and you will end up with a sample that will not only be ideal for the movies, but for the TV networks, magazine covers, record album covers, or any market where star likenesses are a "must."

The Industrial Sample

There's a lot of corporate and industrial work out there, and, if you are going to get your share of it, you must show the art director just how you can handle a typical industrial situation. Why not the oil fields or the factory assembly line combined perhaps with company executives at a shirt-sleeve business conference? Show how you can take a mundane industrial situation and turn it into something exciting and dramatic. The annual report, business magazine, and general industrial markets will love you.

The Product Sample

If you are a trained and specialized product illustrator or photographer (and there are such people), then your portfolio will be packed with product shots or art samples to match any product situation and overwhelm any client.

If you are a general illustrator or photographer, you may overlook the product sample. And yet a good product sample can tilt the portfolio into an entirely new area for you.

Don't just shoot or paint a bottle of soda or a cigarette package or a car. (The specialized product illustrator will get that kind of work.) Put your product in a different environment or in a very atypical situation. Keep the emphasis on the product — by all means, maintain that product's integrity — the client will be watching carefully to make sure his product is not distorted. But do show your imagination and flair in handling products.

The Editorial Sample

The magazines buy a wide range of subject matter — boy and girl, lonely men and women, single women alone — all in specific situations that relate to particular fiction articles. You can let your emotions go when you do this sample, and it will show the magazine art director how you handle sensitive situations with taste and feeling.

The "Slice-of-Life" Sample

Here's the American Family — Mom, Dad, kids, grandparents, and even the family turtle — living a typical Normal Rockwell Americana situation. Just look at the television commercials today and watch the "slice-of-life" situations come to life. These are perfect advertising samples for almost any mass-produced and mass-merchandised product — from hamburgers to soft-drinks to shoes.

These eight basic areas, at least one sample in each category, will give you minimum coverage in some of the prime markets. To these eight basic categories you should add from two to six other noncommercial samples that give an idea of the creative you. The reason for this "formula" approach to the portfolio is that a majority of jobs will fall into predictable and specific areas. While the art director has to know how you think and function as an artist, he also has to be sure that you can do his assignment, which often is of a practical and predetermined nature. Anything you can do, of course, to raise his job from the mundane to the splendid, while still retaining the basic purpose of the assignment, which is to sell goods and services, will make you more desirable to the art director.

Remember that in a majority of cases, you are dealing with everyday people and not exotic personalities. Or you are dealing with goods that are packaged and labeled in an ordinary way. If you start with these hard-core samples (eventually, you will have a number of versions of each), and add your creative input, you will start to find that your portfolio will have a true commercial direction.

If possible, do your samples in full color. It's more dramatic, and, also, the majority of jobs are in color. When talking palette, there is a rule of thumb that says: The advertising palette is "up" because advertising is a hard-sell area while editorial has more room for muted or moody palettes.

"Up" usually means "high-key" lighting. The exceptions are some pharmaceutical advertisements where a specific mood may be required, and beauty photography where muted lighting is needed to dramatize the model's face and keep the emphasis on the cosmetics.

In other words, hard-sell generally is "up"; soft-sell is not.

It is more practical to gear your portfolio to the advertising market since the editorial market will more readily accept an advertising portfolio than vice-versa. It is not uncommon for a client to "type-cast" an editorial book, and unfortunately, as a result, the owner of the editorial portfolio will not get the job.

Ideally, your portfolio should reflect a good mix of editorial and advertising pieces which you can interchange at will depending upon the market you are calling on. But if you can present only one look, the advertising look offers more flexibility and mass-market application.

If possible, somewhere along the line, you should try to get a few black and white samples in your portfolio. When an art director commissions black and white photography, he is usually thinking newspaper, so reproduction is critical. Certain items like food reproduce poorly in newsprint, so pick only black and white subject matter that eliminates reproduction problems.

A word about tailoring the portfolio to a specific client:

When you make that general sales call, you will have a portfolio that shows your photographic or illustrative range, so that the art director can view your total experience and competence as a free-lancer. But there will be opportunities when you can tailor your portfolio to a specific sales call or a specific art director working on a particular account. If the art director is working on a tire account, then load up with every auto or related shot or illustration you have ever done in your life (provided they are up to your standards). If there are animals involved (a dog food account is a natural), then bring in those happy dogs romping on the front lawn — as many as you can find. Art directors love to look at portfolios that are creative, imaginative, and very well produced, but they absolutely go ecstatic over one that specifically fits their needs. Remember: In today's market, art directors must not only sell their bosses — the creative directors and account people — on your talent, but the client as well, and the more help you can give that art director, the better chance he or she has of selling your portfolio. Although it may not always be possible to put together a "selling portfolio for every season", if the opportunity arises, grab it.

One last word about the general portfolio.

Every shot or illustration in your portfolio should be a "stopper." The shot should literally stop the art director visually. It must be commercially-oriented but with the unique approach that only you can provide. Your samples have to "talk" to that art director. They have to make him want to buy from you. The art director has to feel you can handle his problem beautifully and efficiently, sell his client's goods, and make him look good.

If you can produce those "stoppers" constantly, you may start causing excitement in the industry. In the final analysis, consistent "stoppers" are what separate the superstars from the masses.

THE PHOTOGRAPHER'S PORTFOLIO

To be frank, the art director, in many cases, is going to type-cast the photographer. The photographer is either a still-life, people, industrial, travel, or fashion photographer. This is especially true of the large metropolitan markets where there are many photographers, and the art director can have a wide choice in any one specialty.

In smaller markets, most photographers have a range and will shoot everything from industrial to fashion. But since these large metropolitan markets are the most profitable, the special photographic needs and requirements of these markets deserve a closer look.

The Still-Life Photographer

This kind of photographer must usually show how he or she shoots a variety of subjects — metals (silverware, jewelry, etc.), cosmetics (industrial and packaging), liquids (liquors and soft drinks), cigarettes, and, quite often, food.

If you are a still-life photographer, it is a good idea to include a few standard shots that the art director will recognize instantly. For example, liquor shots always include the bottle and glass with the bottle label prominent. It's a good idea to have a few variations of this shot in your portfolio. All the "standards" should be treated in the same way.

However, it is a good idea to have experimentals in your portfolio as well. A variation of the standard industrial still life (perhaps a drill press in an unusual setting?) might cause some excitement. Or what about taking the predictable food still life — which you probably already have in your portfolio — and turning it into an unrealistic, stylized food shot (fifteen scoops of ice cream on a cone?). In other words, show the art director you can handle the "standards," but also show him that you can do some different "knockout" shots if he gives you the chance.

Since the still-life photographer so often gets involved with those bread-and-butter items — catalogs — there should be something indicating how you would handle a department store or merchandise catalog — essentially, volume-shooting in the least amount of time in as attractive a setting as possible. Perhaps you can build a set that can be shot from many angles to show off a variety of products, and yet use the same lighting.

Again, do the standards, but keep those "stopper" shots coming.

The People Photographer and the Fashion Photographer

Although the people and fashion photographer are separate specialties, what separates the "superstar" people photographer and the fashion photographer is the casting of models.

For example, some people photographers specialize in "man-on-the-street" casting while others go for unusual-looking models.

The real comers are usually very attuned to what will constitute a new look in beauty and fashion. These photographers are the first ones to use tomorrow's superstar models.

What makes for good casting with one photographer as compared to bad casting with another photographer? Well, that's like trying to tell a person how to get sex appeal. The photographer whose casting and use of models is consistently outstanding — this talent becomes his selling trademark.

Many mediocre photographers mistakenly think that by taking a beautiful model to the United Nations Building and shooting her in the sunset, they have created a fashion shot that will get them business. Or by hiring a male and female model and shooting them in a fancy restaurant, they have a "slice-of-life" shot.

Casting remains one of those very subtle areas that really does require a trained eye and a sixth sense. The truly good fashion and people photographer will have a definite point of view and will know exactly what he or she is trying to accomplish with each shot. It is really only by knowing themselves that these photographers will know how to cast their shots dramatically as well as commercially.

What shots should the people photographer have in his or her portfolio?

Depending upon your casting, "slice-of-life" situations must be part of your people portfolio. All age groups must be covered: children, elderly folks, young marrieds, business executive-types, housewives, people with animals, etc. There should be a good mix of studio as well as location shots. Attention must be paid to wardrobe, especially if you are reconstructing a period piece (an early 1950's scene, for example).

The good people photographer should also have access to good locations (where can you find a special brick driveway for that bicycle shot or a two-hundred-year-old house for that pharmaceutical shot?). The same is true for the fashion photographer when choosing locations. Fashion photographers must have great exotic scenes or locations at their fingertips. In fact, most fashion (and people) photographers keep their own files of locations. If you happen to see an exotic location in your area (a pyramid in Cincinnati?), shoot it and save it for reference at some later date. If you can use an exotic location that is "local," the New York art director may be interested. It could save him money.

It also doesn't hurt for a people or fashion photographer to have a celebrity portrait in the portfolio. If you can't get a job shooting a celebrity, shoot one free, just for the sample. A celebrity sample picture in your portfolio will help reassure the network or record company art director when he calls upon you to shoot a "big star."

Additional thoughts on fashion photography.

You as a fashion photographer will probably have women's fashion in your portfolio simply because, proportionately, there is more women's fashion around than anything else. Once you've solved the critical problem of casting, lighting becomes important. After all, your fashion photography is there to sell a product. This is especially true when shooting for the clothing manufacturer who must see every single pleat in his piece of merchandise.

On the other hand, a department store is usually much more interested in projecting an image, so every fold in every garment is not as important. Since you should be aiming for a broad spectrum of markets, your portfolio should contain well-lit and beautifully composed samples of both areas.

Accessories are important, too. This is where a good stylist — someone who literally "styles" the surroundings for your shot — is worth his or her weight in gold. It may be worth the money to hire a stylist just to work with you on the setup. A good stylist will have access to clothing and furs, etc. Clothes may not make the man but they can certainly make the right shot. It is not uncommon to run a shot around an original dress or exotic fur piece to create a dramatic "stopper" shot.

The Beauty Market Photographer

One usually says "beauty-and-fashion" photography all in one breath, and, while the two areas are indeed intertwined, beauty shots do have certain distinctions all their own.

First of all, beauty shots are usually head shots, since it is the client's cosmetics and allied products that are being promoted.

Secondly, in casting beauty shots, the photographer must be aware of the types of girls that different cosmetic companies use. There will be a "Revlon" girl or an "Estee Lauder" girl or an "Elizabeth Arden" girl. Each company has its own look and approach to the market. Ideally, you, as a beauty photographer, should create your own "look" and not emulate "looks" that are readily identifiable with the large cosmetic companies.

The best possible make-up artists and hairdressers should be used, since both are important to a great beauty shot.

One should also keep in mind the age of the audience the cosmetic company is trying to reach. Lately, with the female population getting older, much of the new beauty advertising appeals to women over thirty. The age limit will continue to rise simply because the market for cosmetics will be larger in the over-forty groups than under thirty.

Finally, you should have a good mix of black and white beauty photography in your portfolio since there is a large amount of collateral promotional material produced by the large cosmetic manufacturers.

The Annual Report Photographer

While the regular people photographer must develop his sense of casting, the annual report photographer faces the challenge of taking unprofessional models in workaday situations and creating professional shots.

The good annual report photographer is the kind of photographer who generally likes people, has a good sense of design, and infinite patience to make the "hard-hat" plant manager or worker feel at ease while posing.

The annual report photographer must also have a designer's eye for turning a pile of industrial pipe into a beautiful sculpture.

In pulling together a portfolio in this area, it would be a good idea to go to a local manufacturing plant and offer to give them some free photographs in return for letting you have access to their people and physical operation.

Once again, while it's always good to have those standard industrial or annual report shots in the portfolio (the executives around the conference table, etc.), at least a third of your portfolio should have your own distinctive "look" — your artistic view of the ordinary.

Just about every library has a collection of annual reports and a few afternoons spent browsing through these should give you a good idea of what is happening in the annual report market. One last word here. While some annual reports use illustration (and here's where your industrial sample comes in handy), most annual reports use photography, although at times the two might be combined. The annual report market can give you steady income if you can merchandise your portfolio toward it. It is also one of the few markets for a photographer (travel is another) where you do not need a studio, since most shooting is done on location. That fact should be most attractive to the photographer just starting out in the business.

One final word about pulling together a portfolio. It is a hard job. There is no deadline to urge you on. But it must be done — and done well.

Putting together a selling portfolio is a solitary, and sometimes expensive, process (particularly if you are a photographer), and yet it is the most important thing you will ever do. It can help you expand your existing markets, and, if you wish, it can change the whole direction of your career. It can help you revitalize your own creative sparks and get you moving onto the next higher creative plateau. Continually changing your portfolio to make it more saleable will enhance your opportunities to increase your income.

There is no such thing as a perfect portfolio. There will always be market areas that you are not working in, but want to pursue. Or there will be current markets where you are just a step or two from seriously competing with the superstars. The portfolio must be a continually growing entity. Certain pieces will always remain "classics" in your portfolio and will have a timeliness to them that will always make them saleable. But the truly creative person will want to add constantly to his "inventory," not only to help him crack new markets, but to show the world his own artistic growth.

Remember: The portfolio is really you. It is the summary of your creative talent and your technical expertise. It is commercial, but it is also unique, as you are unique. It is your continual passport to new and exciting creative and successful free-lance worlds.

On the following pages are samples of typical illustration and photography portfolio samples that show the various kinds of subject matter you will need to sell consistently in today's competitive market. Obviously, you will bring your own talent and imagination and expertise to each and every piece you produce for your portfolio, but the subject matter should be consistent with what is shown on the following pages.

CREDITS

Illustrations
Boy/Girl: Bob Clarke
Travel: Bob Clarke
Paperback: Jim Dietz
Movie: Robert Hunt
Industrial: Glenn Harrington
Product: Ron Barry
Slice of Life: Jim Dietz
Editorial (Girl with French Horn): Robert Hunt
Pharmaceutical market: Sonja Lamut/ Nenad Jakesevic
Sport Sample (Man playing golf): Glenn Harrington
Fashion: Jackie Jasper
Stopper: Sonja Lamut/ Nenad Jakesevic

All photography samples
By Larry Kerson

Illustration

The Boy-In-Love-With-Girl Sample is perfect for the advertising and magazine market. Casting the ideal boy and girl to suit the moment is critical.

The Travel Sample should capture the fun of places and events, creating the right environment for selling a product.

The Paperback Sample must telescope the plot or key events in a cover image that will attract the reader in a matter of seconds.

Movie Poster art, like mass-market paperbacks, must grab the moviegoers' attention and get them into the theater. The "Plot on the Poster" approach also shows the illustrator's design skill in working with a number of different elements in the same space.

The Industrial Sample that puts the company's best foot forward is an ideal portfolio piece for the illustrator who wants to exploit the advertising and corporate markets.

The Specialized Product Sample contains the "Magic" to transform a simple product into something "more real than real."

The "Slice-of-Life" Sample creates a sense of Americana that makes any product much more acceptable and buyable.

A wonderful example of the Editorial Sample that focuses on mood and event. A reader seeing this illustration just has to read the adjacent article about the girl. And the editorial illustration is designed to create just that reaction.

Pharmaceutical Market Samples don't have to be gory to be good. This piece combines product and lettering—an added "plus" for the illustrator—all wrapped up in a mood that sells.

The Sports Sample may be presented to potential clients in a wide variety of markets, not just to sports magazines or to manufacturers of sport-specific products. While not appropriate for all sales calls, a couple of good sports samples in the illustrator's total portfolio can often pay big dividends.

Fashion is fickle, and the illustrators who want to work in this market must show what they can do. Fashion illustration styles can range from the very realistic to the very loose, and fashion art directors are always interested in seeing new ideas. Portfolio samples for the fashion market are unique, and usually won't be found in any general sales call portfolio.

The Stopper—every portfolio should have one— that breaks new ground and shows how illustrators think and create. Here is a sample that combines a very classical look with modern technology, and one that is sure to get the attention of the art director. Illustrators who combine this kind of dramatic and beautifully designed "artistic" piece with good, hard-sell, market-oriented portfolio pieces separate themselves from the crowd.

Photography

An experimental still-life photograph that turns the ordinary Product Shot into a "Stopper."

An Editorial Photograph that creates an environment for the specific purpose of setting a mood.

Turning the ordinary annual report Product Shot into a stunning and creative selling situation.

A "slice of life" situation done photographically for a national advertiser.

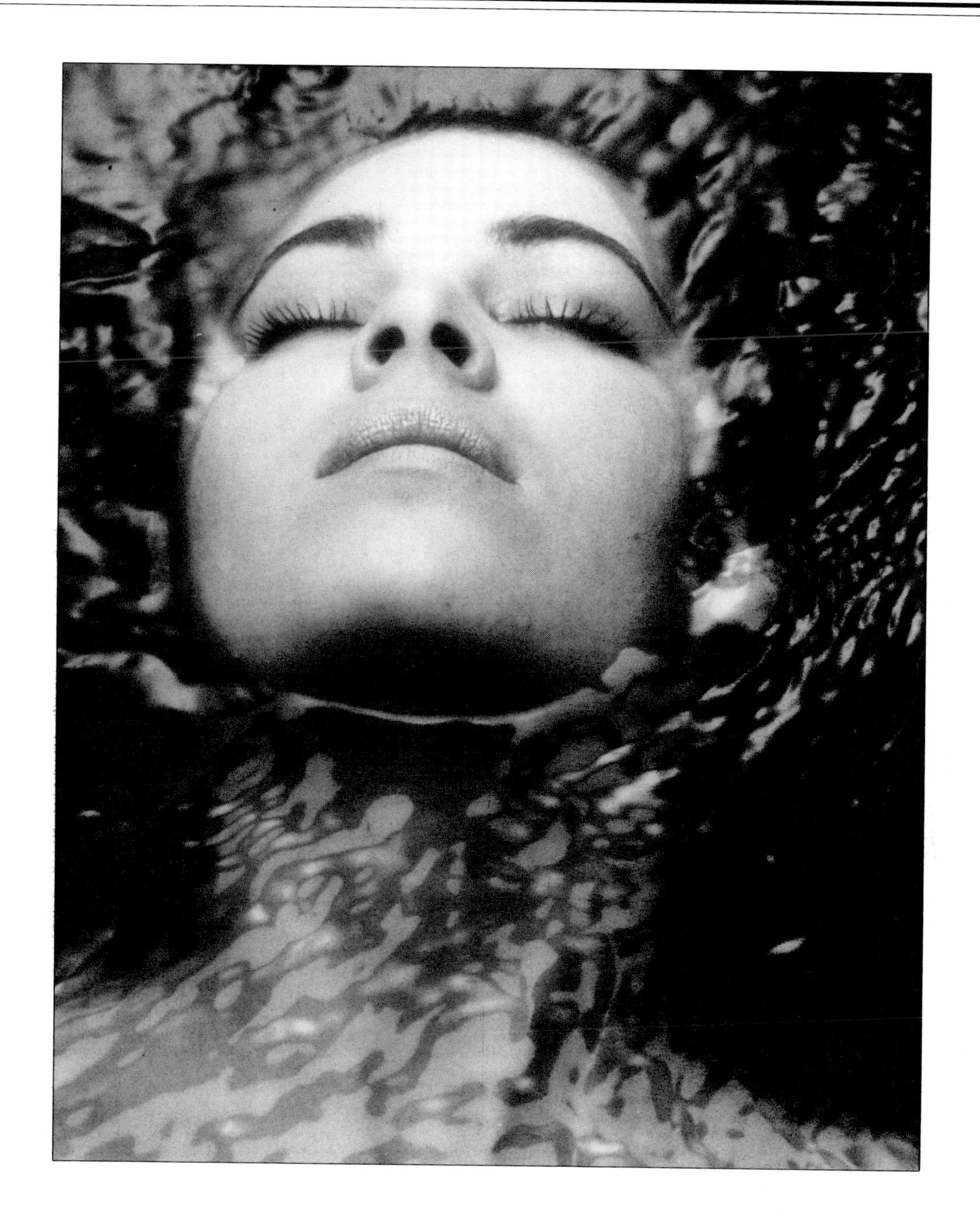

This Beauty and Fashion Photograph highlights a superb model in a dramatic setting.

An effective Boy/Girl Photograph means choosing the right models and establishing a sense of romance.

Promoting and Selling the Artist and Photographer 3

The Value of Promotion

You can be the most gifted and talented illustrator or photographer in the business today, but if nobody knows it, then what good does all that talent do you?

Quite frankly, the difference between a truly successful talent and an "also ran" is promotion. After all, you work in an advertising and communications field. Shouldn't the commercial artist, photographer, or designer advertise and promote his or her abilities? Shouldn't you, trying to make your living in the communications industry, communicate information about your abilities, skills, and accomplishments?

Of course you should. You as an artist/photographer/designer/independent businessman should take your cue from the major advertisers of this world and do what they do. They keep their names in front of their buying public and keep repeating their selling message over and over. This does not happen by chance. It is a planned, image-making selling process and you, the professional free-lancer, must start thinking along those lines. Your promotions and mailings are your "silent sales force," always reminding the art director of your presence, your talents, and your availability.

From another point of view: on any given day, there are literally tens of thousands of prospects for your talents (just in the area where you live, there can be anywhere from a few hundred to a few thousand). These prospects are obviously not buying all of the time, but they are buying some of the time. Also, in agency situations, assignments and accounts can change as needs change, sometimes almost weekly. Physically, even if there were enough hours in the day, you could not possibly call on all of the prospects in your immediate area and even if you could, the chances are that some of them may have changed status or accounts since your initial call. Also bear in mind that the art director is bombarded every day by competitive talents. A week after the art director has seen you, and probably when he's ready to buy, your portfolio is a dim memory, simply because the human brain can only store visual impressions for a certain length of time. You may be perfect for the job — but you're not there and someone else is. So you lose the job — not because you're not talented, or not capable of doing the job, but simply because you got lost in the crowd of talents competing for the art director's attention.

This is where your "silent sales force," your promotion or ad, can make a significant difference. When the buying decisions are made and your monthly promotion or ad is visible, there is every possibility that you will be at least in the running for the job, and all things being equal, you'll probably get it. Your promotion piece can also be used as a leave-behind on your sales call (this area is covered in greater detail later in this section). But make no mistake. The promotion or advertising piece is not a substitute for the direct sales call, but something to be used in conjunction with the sales call. Remember: when selling your talents you must always think in terms of the total selling effort, and advertising and promotion is part of that selling effort.

Statistically, you may find that you can make anywhere from ten to thirty sales calls a week (in metropolitan areas, where many agencies are in one building, the range can be higher than in areas where clients are spread out and one must get involved with travel time). Out of those calls, there probably will be an average of one that will give you a job. This is only an average figure; you can cite instances of making five calls and getting five jobs. However, if you added up all of your personal calls for the year and took an average, you'd probably find that one in twenty produced a job. Bear in mind that personal calls, under the best of circumstances, are a slow way to sell. Through promotion, however, you can do a 5,000 piece mailing in one week. Even if you get only a one percent return on the mailing, that's fifty job possibilities. So you can see the difference.

One other factor is very important, particularly if you are representing yourself. While you are in the studio doing the jobs, you cannot be out on the street making calls. The busier you get, the fewer calls you make. But your "silent sales force" — those promotion pieces of yours — can always be out there working for you. Although promotion pieces may not be the whole answer, they are a reasonable alternative to no one being out in the marketplace on your behalf.

Let's discuss now the pros and cons of some of the different forms of advertising and promotion available to you.

MAGAZINE TRADE ADVERTISING

Some of the positive aspects are: Magazines have an active buying audience — people who normally pay to receive what is in these magazines. Their distribution is guaranteed. There is a one-time cost to you. You do not have to pay for distribution and postage. If you advertise on a multiple basis, you can get special rates. You can also take advantage of special issues (photography or illustration issues, etc.); people usually keep these issues for years, so your advertisement (theoretically) may have a long life as well. You can, for a premium, request special positioning in the magazine where your advertisement will receive the highest impact (the inside front cover or the back cover, for example). If you're on a limited budget, you can arrange for a small space black and white advertising program at a minimum cost. If the magazine is well thought of by its readers, you may benefit from its good reputation. Success is often contagious.

However, there are some negative

aspects to magazine advertising and you should be aware of them. Sometimes you are paying for parts of the magazine's audience that you really don't need. For example, you probably don't want to advertise to your fellow artists or photographers (after all, they are competitors). But many of them will be readers of the magazine in which you advertise. Also, full-color advertisements can be expensive and may not guarantee results. Your promotion schedule is fixed. You are dependent on the magazine's publication date, and you must submit your advertisement well in advance of that. Nevertheless, the advantages of trade magazine advertising far outweigh the disadvantages, and magazines must play an important part in your promotion.

DIRECT MAIL

There are many promotional "plusses" for the use of direct mail. First, a direct mail campaign can be timely and fast, because it is not ruled by other people's closing dates. Black and white mailers can be printed quickly and economically. If you have a new sample of work in your portfolio that you want to show to the marketplace immediately, direct mail can make that possible. Or you might want to do a selective mailing. Let's suppose that you just did an especially good shot of an automobile that you want your buying public to know about. You could pull those automobile clients from your mailing list and do a mailing to that segment of the list. These small, selective mailings are inexpensive but can bring in high returns.

You've probably already guessed the negatives of direct mail. The first is the high cost of postage (going up every single year). The second is the expense and complexity of keeping an active, working mailing list up-to-date — an out-of-date mailing list is of absolutely no value. But don't let these negatives stand in your way. Direct mail can pay off nearly every time you use it.

DIRECTORIES

There are now a great number of national and regional commercial directories where the free-lancer can advertise (A special listing of these directories as well as magazines is included in the back of this book).

There are many advantages to the use of these directories. One, certainly, is guaranteed distribution. The publishers of these directories have taken the burden of compiling a mailing list off your shoulders. Also, there is a one-time space charge and no postage or distribution costs.

And these commercial directories (*American Showcase* and *Black Book* are just two such examples) have, over the years, gained complete acceptance by art directors and art buyers throughout all aspects of the industry and are used on a daily and continual basis. The cost of advertising in these directories is steadily rising, but they do represent an important investment for every free-lance illustrator or photographer.

In addition to the commercial directories, many nonprofit organizations put out award directories which reproduce the winning entries in the various shows and competitions run during the year (The New York Society of

Illustrators Annual Show Directory is a perfect example of this kind of book). These award books are eagerly pored over by potential clients throughout the world because, often, these directories showcase the very best in art and photography (If you are lucky to be in one of these award directories, an advertisement in that same book would be a great way to give you double advertising impact). Advertising page rates in these books are usually much lower than the commercial directories, and, like all directories, clients keep them around for a very long time as a buying reference.

The negative side of directories is that everyone receiving a directory may not be a potential client, so there will be some waste circulation. Also, some of these directories are quite expensive and require payment in advance, so the artist or photographer must often tie up a considerable amount of money for a full year before the directories are distributed.

Directories are usually put out once a year, so you are pretty much locked into the samples that you did at least a year ago. Placement of your advertisement and the quality and quantity of the other advertisers in the directories are also not within your control, and you may not like your position in the book or in relation to the particular advertisements that surround your page or pages.

Every free-lancer should take advantage, within budget limitations, of all these promotional tools. Just as most major advertisers use print, radio, TV, and direct mail to get their message across to the consumer, you — as a successful free-lancer — should also have a program that includes magazines, direct mail, and directory advertising.

MAILING LISTS

No matter what direction your promotion and advertising program takes, everyone needs a client mailing list. The question is: How do you get one?

Compiling a good mailing list is hard work and requires some imagination, but here are some good places to start:

The Standard Directory of Advertising Agencies

This is the "bible" of the advertising business and is a must for any artist or photographer who wants to crack the advertising market. Commonly called "The Redbook," it is available (surprise!) in your local public library or may be purchased from the publisher (National Register Publishing Co., 5201 Old Orchard Road, Skokie, Illinois 60077). The "Redbook" contains names and addresses of all the major advertising agencies throughout the country as well as the accounts they handle (what a help it is if you are an illustrator who does pretty people— the last person you want to call on is the art director on a tire account). Not all of the art directors in an agency will be listed in the "Redbook" — only the top people — but one quick phone call to the art buyer at the agency or the secretary of the head art director can get you the names of the art directors on staff. Don't be afraid to use the telephone to get that kind of information. Agencies are very happy to supply art director names because it means that the agency will be exposed to more talent — both illustrative and photographic — which gives them more options when they buy. Your local Yellow Pages will also supply you with the names of advertising agencies in your town, but the "Redbook" will give you more information about the agencies and make your selling and promotion easier.

The Standard Directory of Advertisers
This is the companion book to the *Advertising Agency Redbook*, and it is also available in your local public library or may be purchased from National Register Publishing Co., 5201 Old Orchard Road, Skokie, Illinois 60077. This book contains the names of all major corporations in the country, their product lines, trademark names, and the names of their advertising agencies, as well as the names of key executives in each company, including the advertising and public relations managers. Normally corporate art directors are not listed, but often there is a corporate creative director or director of corporate communications included who should be on your list. This directory is perfect for the artist or photographer interested in the annual report market, or the in-house corporate graphic market. Also, it's a good idea to keep corporate clients aware of what you're doing, since they sometimes make referrals to their agencies based on the promotions they receive.

The Literary Market Place
Here is a book, containing all of the names and addresses of hard-cover, paperback, and magazine publishers in the country, that is available through your local library. Or you can purchase it through the publisher, R.R. Bowker Co., 1180 Avenue of the Americas, New York, New York 10036. The book contains the names of art directors and key promotional people involved in the various departments of the major magazine and publishing houses.

The Working Press of the Nation
This is the overall title of a series of separate directories which may be at your local library or obtained through National Research Bureau, 424 North 3rd Street, Burlington, Iowa. The five separate directories put out by this company are:

THE NEWSPAPER AND ALLIED SERVICES DIRECTORY, which includes the exclusive listings of newspapers, news services, newsreels, and photo services for all major newspapers in the United States and Canada. It is a directory primarily directed to the personnel in the major editorial markets of these newspapers.

THE MAGAZINE AND EDITORIAL DIRECTORY contains listings for people in all areas for over 4,500 magazines.

THE RADIO AND TELEVISION DIRECTORY lists the names of local programming personnel in the major radio and television stations throughout the country.

THE FEATURE WRITER AND SYNDICATE DIRECTORY contains the names of over 900 leading feature writers who appear regularly in the top national

Some Quick Questions and Answers about Mailing Lists

Should you hire a professional mailing house to service your list and do all your mailings?

Yes, if you are going to mail out promotional material on a very regular basis (at least once a month). But if you are going to send out one mailing a year, then getting a mailing house involved just doesn't make sense. Get your girl or boyfriend, or your wife or husband, to type and stamp the envelopes and mail out the pieces. Mailing houses will charge you by the piece mailed, and that can be expensive. Sometimes good old fashioned "sweat," particularly if you are new to the business, is the best way to get a mailing done. And there are particular advantages to doing the mailing yourself. You will learn quickly the right and wrong way to do things. You will become quite familiar with the list, and you can control exactly what you are going to send out and to whom.

On the other hand, as previously mentioned, if you do a tremendous amount of promotion, it makes sense to hire a mailing house to do the whole job. You, as an illustrator or photographer, should spend all your time shooting or painting. A good mailing house can take the mailing burden off your mind.

How often should you mail during a year?

The standard answer to that question is that there is no answer. If you have something important to say to all of the art directors on your list all the time, then bombard them with at least a mailing a month. On the other hand, if you are new to the business, one major, well-planned mailing might show off what you do to the best advantage, and keep on working for you all year long.

What about specialized mailings as compared to big mass-market mailings?

Let's suppose you have photographed an absolutely sensational piece of jewelry. It makes no sense to send that out to forty thousand art directors, ninety-nine percent of whom work on accounts that have absolutely nothing to do with the jewelry business. Instead a very selective mailing to key department store or jewelry specialty shop art directors might just get you work — and at far less than what a mass mailing would have cost you.

Quite frankly, because of the high volume of mail pouring into every art director's office, specialized or selective mailings are being used much more by both illustrators and photographers with much more effective results.

magazines as well as a listing of leading free-lance photographers available for work throughout the country. As a photographer, you might want to investigate the possibility of having yourself included as one of these free-lance photographers.

THE GEBBIE HOUSE MAGAZINE DIRECTORY contains detailed information on virtually all of the major house organs of over 4,000 United States corporations, government agencies, and other groups. The house organ is an excellent market for both illustration and photography, and this particular directory should be an important source.

Mailing lists can also be purchased from many of the magazines serving the art director market at a charge which is fairly minimal and is usually based on so much per thousand names. These mailing lists usually contain all the subscribers to the magazine, but you may request special customer lists put together by the magazine for sale to outsiders.

In addition, the Art Directors' Club in most cities will sell its mailing list to an illustrator or photographer. Because this list contains active members of the Club, it represents a very good direct mail investment.

One word of caution about mailing lists. Because of the nature of the advertising and promotion business, personnel turnover can be significant. When doing any mailing, always include a return address. This will automatically help you eliminate all those people who no longer work in the business. Secondly, continually verify (and update) your mailing list with each advertising agency's art buyer. Remember: Promotions cost you money. You should always make sure that the mailings are reaching those art directors who are in the business and buying today. Maintaining a mailing list is hard work, but is truly the key to a successful direct mail program.

So, now you've got your direct mail distribution list in shape, and you are all set for action. What's next? Well, what do you mail? Let's take a look at the many different kinds of promotional pieces you can produce — all of which will generate business for you.

PROMOTION MAILERS

The most effective and commonly used type of promotion piece is the mailer. This mailer can be full-color (the most desirable and expensive) or black and white. For the beginning illustrator or photographer, a black and white mailer can be just as effective as a color mailer as long as it dramatically shows what you do. Remember one very simple truth about the free-lance business: Any kind of mailer is better than no mailer at all.

Fold-Out

One of the most effective designs — in either black and white or color — is the fold-out mailer. This mailer contains five to seven panels approximately five inches wide and printed either on one side or two, depending upon how much money you want to spend. Each panel contains samples of your work which quickly shows exactly what you do and how you do it. This fold-out mailer fits easily into a standard #10 envelope and can be mailed to the art director very efficiently.

The major advantage of this fold-out mailer is that it is almost a mini-portfolio, showing a variety of subject matter and emphasizing your range. The fold-out mailer can be conveniently placed in the art director's promotion file for future reference. After all, the easier you make it for the art director to inventory your promotion piece, the better chance you will have of being considered seriously for a future project. Keeping your promotion piece out of that art director's wastebasket should always be one of your key objectives.

The only real disadvantage to the fold-out mailer is that the individual subjects on each panel are considerably reduced from actual size, which might diminish the impact of the piece. But if the art director likes what you are doing, no matter what size the printed sample may be, he or she will call for your portfolio, which is really the purpose of any promotion piece.

Posters

At one time, posters were one of the most effective means of promotion available to photographers and illustrators. All art directors enjoyed receiving posters, and most hung them for decoration and ready reference. Posters always showed the photographer or illustrator to the very best advantage.

Unfortunately, because of the tremendous cost of reproducing posters and mailing them, as well as the lack of usable wall space in most art directors' offices, they are now less popular. If it is possible, at least one poster should be created that makes a major statement about your work. However, it is not an essential part of your promotional arsenal and has become a luxury to most people in the graphic-arts business.

Oversized Mailers

A mailing piece is not restricted to a small, fold-out format. Mailers can be produced in almost any size desired. However, whether you produce your promotional pieces in black and white or in color, do not forget the filing problem. Often, oversized mailers make it too easy for the art director to throw them out.

Small Black and White Promotion Pieces

One of the simplest and least expensive forms of promotion pieces is the small black and white piece. It can usually be done by any black and white printer or quick-copy shop, using original art or photographs. The printer can drop in type and print anywhere from one hundred to thousands. The small black and white piece should also fit into a standard #10 envelope and it should be light enough to require minimum postage. The small black and white piece can be folded to 8 1/2-by-11 inches, printed on one side, or a small post-card size. These pieces are also an excellent "leave-behind" on a sales call. If this piece is all you can afford, don't worry about it. Some high-paying projects have been acquired through a very simple black and white mailing piece.

The Free Promotion Piece

Yes, there is such a thing as a "free" promotion piece and it's called the magazine tearsheet. If you make plans in advance, almost any magazine will make arrangements to give you a quantity of tear sheets of the illustration you created. If you want large quantities, you may have to pay for them, but the cost can be modest. Get a sticker printed up with your name and telephone number on it (a rubber stamp will do just as well), put it on the tearsheet, fold it, and mail it out. In essence, the tear sheet becomes a free, full-color or black and white mailer.

There is also another free promotional possibility. Quite often, an advertiser or printer wants full-color art for use in his poster, calendar, etc., but does not want to spend a lot of money on it. You may be able to swap some of your work in exchange for a quantity of full-color posters or calendars. Arrangements can be made to have your name and address printed right on these posters or calendars. Usually, both parties are very satisfied with this arrangement. The customer gets art or photography that he could not possibly afford otherwise, and you get a beautiful promotion piece.

The Best "Freebie" of Them All...Publicity

Every magazine, every trade paper, is looking for items to fill its pages. Wouldn't you like to have one page, or more, free of charge in a major trade magazine? Well, the possibility exists through publicity, and never overlook it. Naturally, many people are also looking for that "free" exposure, and there's a lot of competition, but it's worth the effort. Every time you do something that you're truly proud of, that's beautiful and noteworthy, send off a copy and a little background on it to the trade press. While the press may not always agree with your interpretation of the importance of what you're doing or may not have space that month, there's always the chance that they will reprint it, giving you full credit. Simply identify who you did the job for (client, agency, art director, etc.) and send it to the magazine. If you're having a significant showing of your work at your local art directors' club, professional society, or gallery, you may want to invite the press to a viewing. Use discretion and send only your best work to the press, but the chances are that if you do this on a consistent basis, someone in the trade press is going to like it and give you some recognition.

THE PERSONAL CALL

Although promotion is extremely important, nothing really beats the personal call that you make on the art director. Having the opportunity to "eye-ball" with the art director, to see his reaction to your work first hand, and to ask him questions about the kinds of accounts he is working on, what prices he is paying, and which competitive photographers or illustrators he is using can provide you with invaluable information.

Unfortunately, getting an appointment with the art director today is very, very difficult. The art director, particularly in the advertising agency, is overworked and overburdened with

Some General Promotion Piece Design and Production Tips

Try to design your promotion piece so that it is light weight. Remember: the purpose of any promotion piece is to show subject and style, not to last for an eternity or win a printing award.

Design the piece so it fits into a standard #10 envelope. Why spend money on special-run, over-sized envelopes to fit those over-sized mailers when a standard mailing will do just as well?

If you are designing a multi-image mailing piece — one that will show a variety of your work at one time — make sure that you not only select a cross-section of your expertise, but also have additional portfolio samples in the same subject-matter area to back it up. The worse thing you can do is to show your full hand, all at once, and go in on the initial call empty-handed, with nothing to show except what is on the mailer.

If you hire a designer to create the mailer, you (or your agent, if you have one) should choose the pieces that go into any mailing piece, not the designer. You know which pieces are getting the best response from art directors and those samples are the ones that will work for you regardless of how they do or don't fit into the overall design. Mailers show style and subject matter, not printing or design expertise (another reason why an inexpensive printer who "gang-runs" your mailers along with other jobs, may, in the long run, be just as effective as the very expensive printer who individually separates every single image so that your art or photography "sings"). If you don't have the samples to show, a good printing job won't help you impress the art director.

Investigate third-class mailing requirements and bulk-rate, particularly if you are doing a great number of promotions or have designed special mailing pieces which might be heavier in weight than standard fold-out mailers. In many cases, third-class mail will arrive at the art director's desk a few days after first class but at half the cost to you.

Finally, don't overlook mailing out the page you took in one of those annual art or photography directories. Normally, those directories will provide you with up to 2,000 free reprints. All you have to do is have them folded so they fit into a #10 envelope and mail them out. The additional mailing will remind buyers and reinforce what is in the directory. Reprints and tearsheets are an economical form of self-promotion available to anyone in the business.

responsibilities, and often the last thing he wants is to spend time with someone who wants to sell him something. In many cases, the art director is handling more than one account and has to "juggle" great numbers of things while doing his job. In other instances, the art director may be responsible for both television and print and spend a great deal of time away from the office shooting television commercials or in meetings planning these television commercials.

Because of these serious restrictions on the art director's time in both the advertising and editorial markets, it is almost a universal requirement that you drop your portfolio off, either on specially appointed days, or at the art director's request. If the agency or magazine insists that you leave the portfolio, by all means do it. The art director actually will have more time to look at and evaluate your work when no one is looking over his shoulder, trying to influence his decision. Dropping a portfolio off is rapidly becoming standard operating procedure. As an artist and photographer, you might as well get used to it. Obviously, it is much better than having no one look at your work at all.

If you want the chance to call on that hard-to-see art director personally, how do you go about getting an appointment and making the most of it? There are no hard and fast rules, but here are some suggestions that might make the job easier.

In getting the appointment, the telephone is your key weapon, and you must make it work for you. Keep in mind that you are not at the top of the art director's list of nice things to do that day, so when you make that telephone call to him, make sure you get to the point in a hurry. Tell him who you are and why you are calling. Try to give him a valid reason why he should give you a personal appointment. Perhaps you have developed a shooting technique that will help the art director on a specific account and save him money. Or maybe you did an illustration for a similar-type account that might interest him. Or, as a last resort, perhaps a friend or co-worker of the art director's has recommended you because he thought you had something to offer. In other words, give the art director a reason for wanting to see you.

Be prompt and don't linger on the phone, stretching out the conversation when the art director wants to get back to work. Don't oversell yourself. If the art director doesn't want to give you an appointment — he may be too busy, he may be on an account that hasn't bought an illustration in twenty years, perhaps he is already using a competitive photographer whom he is happy with and has no intention of replacing, or a million other good reasons — don't try to argue him into an appointment. In the business of free-lance, art directors change accounts continually, and you always want to make sure that the art director thinks positively of you no matter where he is.

If the art director does agree to meet with you, make sure you confirm your appointment with him at least a day in advance. If he does not give you an appointment, but suggests that you call him back in a week or so, follow up with him on schedule. Always thank the art director for talking to you and get off the phone.

Once you have an appointment, it is very important to follow these very simple, common-sense rules (it's amazing how many so-called professionals don't):

- Always be on time. The art director paid you a compliment by granting you an appointment. Don't waste his time by being late. Also, he's likely to think that if you are late for an appointment, you will be late meeting a job deadline. Arriving ahead of schedule, you can organize your sales pitch in your mind and prepare yourself mentally.

- Dress neatly. You are a business professional and should dress like one. This doesn't mean a coat and tie is required. But it does mean that whatever you wear should be neat and clean and contemporary. Just keep in mind that everything about the way you look and act will have a positive or negative effect on the art director.

- Know what you want to accomplish. If it's a general "get-acquainted-with-your-work" kind of call, show the art director an organized sampling of what you do. If it's a specific problem-solving call, quickly tell him how you can help. Don't ramble. Don't waste time. Make every selling minute count.

- There is no such thing as sex appeal on a business call. If you are a man calling on a female art director, don't act cute. She is a professional with a job to do and is not interested in romance — in fact, she will probably take offense. The same holds true if a woman calls on a male art director. You are there to sell a product, namely your illustration or photography. A sales call is no place for any boy/girl games.

- If your samples are not appropriate, ask the art director if he would mind suggesting the names of other art directors in the agency who might be better prospects for your work. If you have acted in a professional manner, he should be more than happy to do so.

- When the interview is finished, thank the art director for his time and give him your promotion piece to keep on file. Never leave an art director's office without placing some kind of reminder of what you do in his hands. Keep in mind that he probably sees hundreds of portfolios and many illustrators and photographers in a week, and it is impossible for him to remember what they all do. A good "leave-behind" promotion piece plus good follow-up mailings will simply increase your odds of getting a job.

- If the art director is impressed with your work and thinks you might be appropriate for a particular project, you may follow up with a phone call a few days later, if you do not hear from him before then. But do not annoy him with continual telephone calls. He probably has to get approval from his creative supervisor, and then the client, so he may not be in a position to assign the job immediately. One follow-up call from you is certainly permissible and acceptable, and the art director almost expects it. What the art director will not expect and will not tolerate is the all-too-frequent, every-other-day call, which succeeds in irritating rather than reassuring and selling him. If you are right for the art director's project, he will invite you back.

OTHER PROMOTIONAL ACTIVITIES

Many other opportunities for self-promotion exist. It's up to you to exploit these to the maximum:

Speak before any kind of group you can. Art director groups are ideal because you have a captive audience of prospects. But any group might contain potential customers. Plus, speaking engagements give you a great chance to issue publicity releases on yourself. Never turn down any chance to speak.

Participate in shows and exhibits. Many advertising agencies, trade organizations, publications, and corporations have exhibition space that they provide free of charge. The space can be as simple as a wall near the art department in an advertising agency, or it can be in a professional gallery, complete with curators and professional publicity. If the space is free, and you meet the criteria of the group providing the space (for example, you must be a member of the Society of Illustrators or you cannot "show"), then by all means hang your illustrations or photography prints. Shows are unpredictable, and, while you are usually allowed to invite certain numbers of your own guests, you can never be sure who will attend. However, if you get one job out of a show, it was well worth the time and effort.

If you have a good selection of mounted prints or framed paintings for use in these shows, you will find that it's a simple matter to "travel" the show from gallery to gallery. Since you are spending money to get your show pieces in order, you should get maximum use from them.

Write letters to art directors, advertising managers — anyone who might be helpful to you. Be inventive. Why not write a little thank you note to that art director who gave you an appointment? If you see something in the paper that might interest a particular person in the industry, clip it out and send it enclosed in a note. Look upon a good letter as a sales call. It can really work for you and costs you practically nothing.

Finally, use any method of promotion — whether an advertising campaign, a mailer, a poster, a telephone call, or a letter — to keep your name before important art directors. Promotion, after all, is simply presenting the obvious over and over again until someone finally gets the message and acts on it.

On the following pages are some examples of effective promotional pieces.

CREDITS: Promotional Pieces
B&W piece: Glenn Harrington
B&W piece: Roy McKie
Fold out mailer: Jim Dietz
Postcard: Judith Cheng
Art Annual tear sheet: Jackie Jasper

Small black and white promotion pieces (actual size of this piece is 4 X 7") can highlight an artist or photographer's latest job or technique very effectively. Every new artist or photographer entering the commercial field should invest in small black and white promotion pieces for use both as an introductory mailer and as a "leave-behind" after a call on an art director.

This black and white, 8 1/2 X 11" promotional piece is informational as well as promotional since it shows a range of subject matter on the same page. It can be easily folded down to fit into a standard #10 envelope. And the cost is minimal.

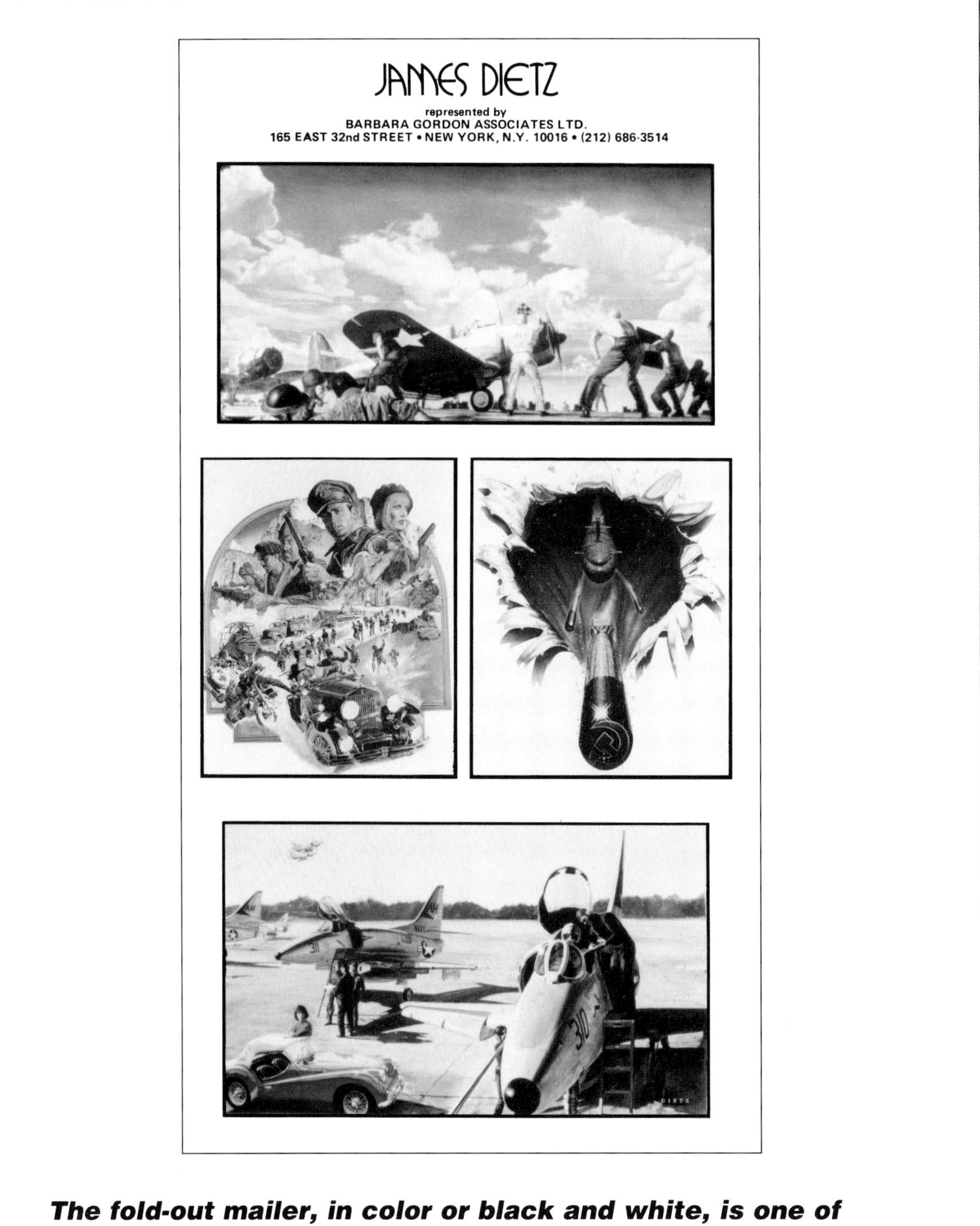

The fold-out mailer, in color or black and white, is one of the more popular promotion pieces used by both artists and photographers. Because several different samples of work can be shown on the same mailing piece, it acts as a mini-portfolio.

The black and white or color postcard (5 1/2 X 3 1/2") is the perfect way to show one good, effective portfolio sample in a format that is easy to produce and easy to mail. Your name, address, and telephone number, plus the name and address of the recipient of the piece goes on the reverse side, turning the postcard into a cost-effective self-mailer. In addition, a postcard serves as an excellent "leave-behind" for your sales calls.

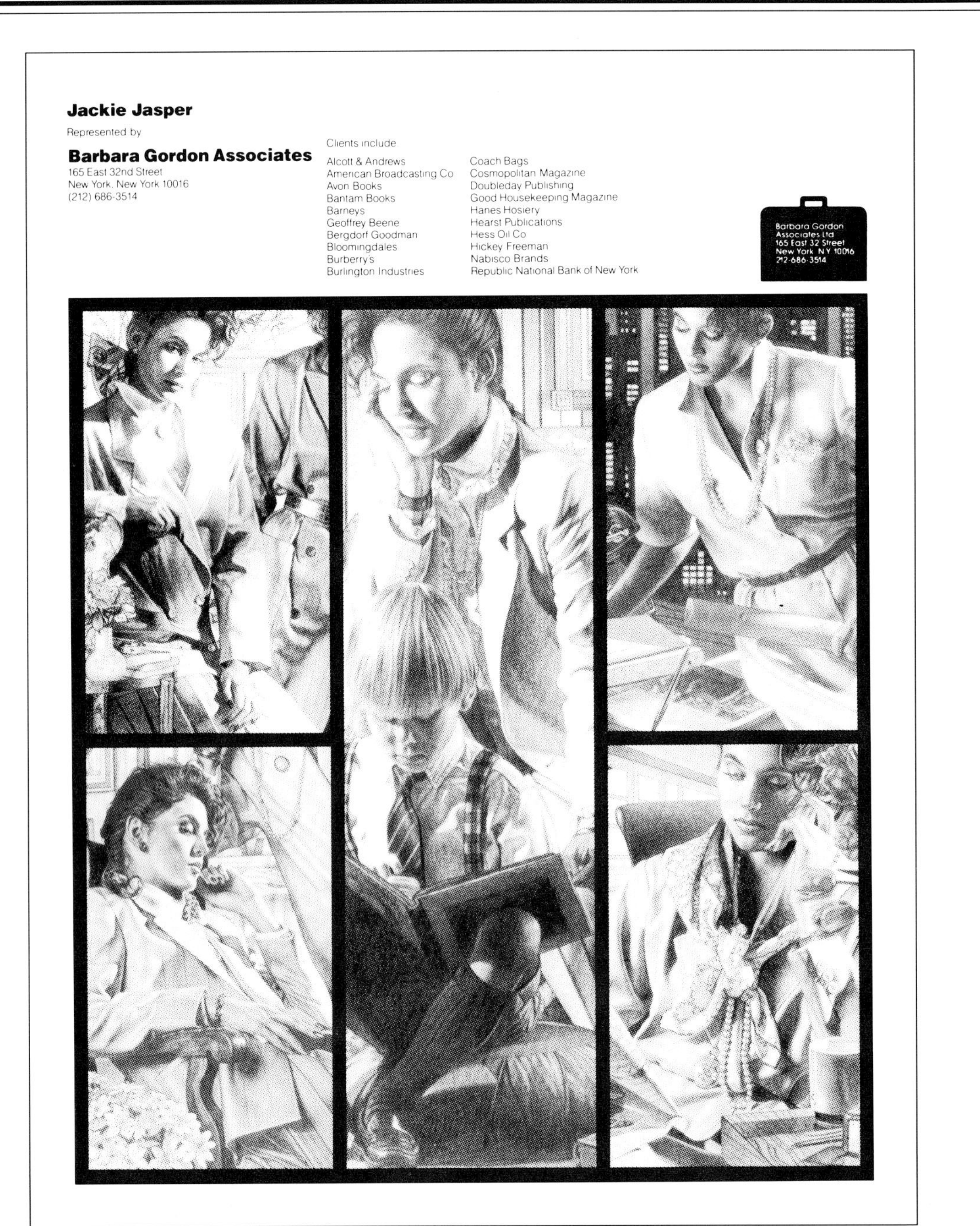

If you advertise in photography and illustration directories, you will generally receive a quantity of your specific page free of charge as part of your advertising contract. These tear sheets make excellent promotional pieces and can also reinforce your advertising efforts.

Pricing—The Fine Art of Negotiation

This is probably the most difficult and controversial subject in the entire industry. That's because any discussion about pricing involves a lot of intangibles.

Today's free-lance marketplace is one of extremes and inconsistencies. There is everything from amateurs who, out of ignorance or desperation, are quoting prices far too low, to "superstars" who can get the equivalent of a year's salary on one job. In between, the variations are limitless.

It is not uncommon to find two art directors in side-by-side offices in the same agency, paying prices thousands of dollars apart for similar jobs. Is one paying too much, or is the other paying too little? The question is really unanswerable. So how does the average free-lancer cope, when even seasoned buyers and sellers are occasionally overwhelmed by pricing inconsistencies? This section will try to set up some criteria to deal with these inconsistencies and to help you price competitively.

Let's start by saying that the only price to give on any job is a fair price. A fair price is the price that guarantees a client the highest quality work at a price that is competitive for the usage intended and that will guarantee the free-lancer a fair profit based on the time and expertise it takes to complete the job.

Before you even contemplate pricing, you should have some idea of how much time it takes you to do a job. Also, consider your regular expenses, such as studio rental, supplies, equipment, taxes, etc. In other words, what are your normal, everyday operating costs for being in business? It is from these costs that you can establish a "minimum." A "minimum" price is one that will cover your expenses and to which you will add a reasonable profit. It is only by being fair to yourself that you will be able to give a fair and reasonable price to your client. Before determining what is fair, you must know your costs.

Giving a fair and reasonable price will help you get repeat business, and repeat business is the stuff that careers are built upon.

The talent who is fair to himself will avoid the temptation to "hose" a client on one job to make up for another job that he underbid. This kind of frivolity in pricing eventually catches up with you because, basically, it is a small business community, and art directors talk to one another. If you keep underpricing jobs, the word will eventually get around that you are "low-balling" jobs, and you'll soon find that you are viewed with suspicion (Can you really deliver a quality job at such a low price?). On the other hand, if you take advantage of the client by quoting high prices, the word gets out that you are "unaffordable," and you may find that the phone suddenly stops ringing.

The majority of art directors are pretty decent people who are interested in spending their client's money properly and effectively. They also realize that you, as a free-lancer, have to live and that, if you are very unhappy with a price, you cannot do your best work.

So, if you start out being professional in your approach to pricing — and that ultimately means being fair — you will run into surprisingly few problems.

THE TEN KEY PRICING QUESTIONS

Here are the ten key questions that should always be asked before pricing any job.

1. The first and most obvious question you must ask is: Just what exactly is the project to be priced? Is it a brochure? A national consumer advertisement? A limited trade ad? A point-of-purchase display? Or a photograph or illustration for a product package? The kind of project you are being asked to price will have a large bearing upon the kind of price you will ultimately give.

2. Is the photograph or illustration color or black and white? It is not necessarily true that a color illustration, for example, will automatically cost more than a black and white. Other factors such as usage may make the latter more expensive. But your time, equipment, and expenses will be more working with color than with black and white, so you must ask this question before you can price the job intelligently.

3. Is the job one single assignment, or part of a campaign? Obviously, if you are going to end up illustrating ten full-page national advertisements for the same client — and you are guaranteed to do all ten — your price to the client is going to be lower on a per-ad basis than if you end up illustrating only one. By the same reasoning, if you have based your price on doing the full campaign, and everything stops after you have completed one or two ads, then a price adjustment upward should be made by the client, provided you have negotiated this contingency at the beginning of the job. Remember when pricing any job: nobody likes surprises.

4. What is the job deadline? If you pick up a job on Friday, and the art director must have it on Monday morning (now you know, as a free-lancer, what happens to your social life), that job must command a higher price than the same job due in four weeks. Establishing a true deadline with the art director is a very important consideration in helping you establish a fair price.

5. How complicated is the job? For example, is it a location shot that will command greater amounts of your time, or just a simple set-up in your studio? Will a great deal of your time be needed to create and plan the shot, or are you working from such a tight layout that even your dog could shoot it? Will it be your responsibility to cast models, approve props, etc., or will this be the responsibility of the client? Will you be forced to spend lengthy creative time thinking about the shot and discussing it with the client before it is approved? (Some photographers, by the way, in this particular situation, will quote what is called a "conference fee" which is over and above any shooting fee. If the client accepts the photographer's idea and gives out the assignment to the photographer, then this "conference fee" is applied to the final shooting fee and not in addition to it.) The point is: Time is money to you, and the complexity or simplicity of the job will very definitely have an effect on your profit and must be part of your pricing strategy.

6. What are the estimated expenses on the job and will they be paid by the client? Expenses play an important part in any price, particularly in photography, and often the photographer will separate his price into several different categories, all of which are estimated before agreement on a fixed price is reached.

The shooting fee actually is the fee that the photographer will receive for shooting the job, and expenses are just that, and a job may hinge on just how much expense money is involved. You should refer to the American Society of Magazine Photographers (ASMP) estimate sheet for an idea of the range of items that can be included in the expense budget. (You'll find a similar form in the Addendum of this book.) Since most expense estimates are given in writing, it is a good idea to use an estimate sheet like ASMP's or to devise one of your own.

In the case of illustration, expenses may include travel, if location illustration or special location reference is required (as an example, if a magazine sends an illustrator out to cover the Super Bowl, the magazine should pick up all the expenses on this — but again, this must be clarified before the illustrator packs his or her bags). Special props or materials are usually billable expenses as well. If the illustrator hires a photographer to shoot models for reference (particularly critical to photorealistic illustrators), both the photographer and the model are part of the expense budget.

A Word of Caution. Do not assume that all expenses are billable, no matter what the situation or what anyone has told you. At the time of accepting the job, you should determine which expenses are billable and which are not. You then should give the art director a realistic estimate of what you believe the expenses might be. These expense estimates should be included on the purchase order. Remember: Clients differ greatly, particularly when it comes to expenses, so always be prepared for the unusual. A client may not bat an eye at paying your round trip airfare to Alaska, but may become enraged over the $7.50 messenger bill that you put on your final bill because you never asked him whether messenger bills were going to be paid or not. Always be very up front about asking which expenses are covered.

7. How is the photograph or illustration going to be used? A big, national, full-color advertisement must cost more than that very same advertisement running in a small, regional magazine with one-tenth the circulation, even though the amount of work you had to do may have been exactly the same. And that black and white newspaper advertisement will be priced a good deal higher if it runs in a national newspaper like *The Wall Street Journal* rather than in your local paper.

Also, are there additional uses involved for that same photograph or illustration? For example, is your client now going to take that same illustration you did for that national advertisement and use it on a coast-to-coast, in-store display? Perhaps the client plans to use it in the company's annual report, or employee newsletter. Each and all of these additional uses of your artwork mean additional money for you — if you think to ask about them. The old days, when a client could commission an illustration or photograph for one specific use and then blatantly use that same art or photograph forever and however he pleased, are over — unless that client is prepared to pay for the right to use the art in anyway he wants. In addition, it is quite common for a client to buy the use of your illustration or photography for a specific period of time (one year is most common). After that time-frame is up, usage rights return to you. If the client wants to continue to use your art or photograph beyond that specified time-frame, again, the client must pay for it.

8. What rights are being sold? A very big question, indeed, when it comes to setting a price. The question of copyright will be covered later in this section, but suffice it to say that the kind of rights your client wants to buy, will materially affect the price that client will ultimately pay. Does the client want to reproduce your art only once? Does he want to reproduce it whenever he decides to and exclusively prevent anyone else from using the same art? Does he want to own the physical art itself, as well as having the right to reproduce it throughout the world? All of these specific conditions will change your price to the client, and must be negotiated by you. Remember, pricing is a step-by-step process. Every single step must be negotiated by you until a fair and reasonable price agreement is reached.

9. What is the client's budget? This is an obvious question to ask and yet it is often ignored and overlooked. Regardless of the circumstances, if the client wants to pay "x" dollars for a particular job, that is what he is going to pay, and the only choice open to you is: do you want to do the job at the client's price, or don't you? If you are dealing with a large national company that spends a great deal of money in television and other areas, then you can assume (although not always correctly), that the photography or illustration budget will be reasonable. On the other hand, some regional clients or local advertisers may not accept, or be able to justify, what may be a very reasonable price on your part for a particular project. They have never paid that kind of money for anything. Nothing is chiseled in stone when it comes to pricing. Some small clients are willing to spend large sums because they want to project a prestigious image. Others want to control costs and will refuse to pay what the project may be worth. Every client has a budget, but remember that a budget is generally nothing more than a client guide to expenses. There are client budgets that are simply unbreakable. Other budgets can be exceeded if you make a good pricing case to the client. The best advice is to go into every pricing situation with an open mind and quote what you believe is a fair and reasonable price for the job regardless of the budget. Just keep in mind that the client pays the bills and always has the final say.

10. Finally, can you afford to do the job you are being asked to price? A very good question, because as a freelancer, you have only so many hours in a day to do a job, and if you are working on a very complicated assignment, you may not have time to work on anything else. So that very complicated job better be paying you enough to make it worth your while. Of course, there are always those jobs that you will do for the experience, or for the portfolio, but you are in a business, and the rent must be paid. Obviously, it is impossible to plan your life weeks in advance, so you won't know that the low-paying job you turned down today, because you decided you could not afford to do it, will be the only job opportunity you will have for the next month. And it never fails that once you commit yourself to that same low-paying job, the floodgates will swing open and every job you ever dreamed about will be available for pricing. That's simply the nature of the business.

A Word about Advances

Often, a photographer will be involved in a shooting that requires spending his own funds to get the project underway. Or an illustrator has to travel to collect research before he begins the painting. It is not uncommon under these circumstances to ask for an advance. The advance is deducted from the final billing. Most big agencies will give an advance almost automatically, but some clients will not. In situations where you must spend an appreciable amount of your own funds, it is becoming more common and acceptable to receive an advance payment.

MARKET PRICE RANGES

It is not wise (or even possible) to quote specific prices for each and every photography or illustration job, since each job is truly different and must be priced on an individual basis. On the other hand, an understanding and awareness of price ranges that currently exist in the commercial art and photography field can help the beginning illustrator or photographer, as well as the seasoned professional, to choose a fair and reasonable price for his or her work.

Every illustrator and photographer should become familiar with the two published price guides listed here that cover virtually all markets:

The Pricing and Ethical Guidelines, published by the Graphic Artists Guild (GAG).

The American Society of Magazine Photographers (ASMP) Business Practices in Photography

Both may be obtained by writing to the above organizations. (Complete mailing addresses may be found in the Addendum of this book.) *The Pricing and Ethical Guidelines* may also be ordered from its distributor, North Light Books, by calling toll free: 1-800-289 0963.

Keeping in mind that prices change — moving both up and down — on an almost constant basis, these price guides are just that: guides to general pricing. They do not represent hard and fast pricing rules, nor are they the final answer to the price that you, as an artist or photographer, should charge. But they will give you an idea of what the industry — your fellow competitors and their customers — considers fair price ranges for a wide variety of photographic and illustrative assignments.

However, most pricing expertise is gained through on-the-job experience pricing a job from start to finish. Price ranges are helpful but they are not a substitute for pricing under actual job conditions.

Remember that the price ranges are most helpful when pricing advertising jobs, where there are no set pricing rules, as compared to editorial jobs, where standard page rates may dictate what price you will receive (more on this later). The pricing guides will relieve some of your anxiety when pricing a job with an advertising agency art director, and should at least keep you competitive.

One very important thought: Everyone makes mistakes from time to time in pricing an advertising job, regardless of how much experience he may have in the field. There will be times when the price you quote is much too low for the amount of work involved, and the art director will gleefully accept your offer and quickly produce a purchase order.

On the other hand, you will lose a job now and then because the price you quoted was just too rich for the client's blood.

The only thing you can do in either one of these situations is to learn from it. Make a promise to yourself to be more careful next time. File the information away for future reference. But don't dwell on it. Pricing mistakes will happen. The secret of good pricing is to make sure you are getting a good, fair, and reasonable price more often than you are getting a bad price. Experience will be your greatest teacher, particularly in the area of advertising market pricing.

What about art and photography for magazines, paperbacks, movies, and other areas?

Magazines

Most magazines have pre-set page rates, as well as cover rates. Prices paid for cover art and photography are generally higher than for art and photography used on the inside of the magazine. However, since magazines do not publish a price list for art and photography, it is always a good idea to ask what the budget is before offering any price. Even though a magazine has a page rate, there is still room for some negotiation (Certainly, this is true for nationally known talents, who can demand higher prices, but you should not be afraid to ask for a price that you feel is fair for the job, regardless of what you may have heard the page rate is). Magazines generally pay prices that are lower than advertising prices, but they still attract illustrators and photographers, primarily because they serve as important "showcases" for creative work.

General Trade Books

General trade book publishers usually have set rates for full color or black and white illustrations, on a per-page basis. In addition, royalties may be paid for art produced in connection with a total book (not just cover art). These royalties are usually paid as advances against future earnings.

Trade book prices are usually lower than paperback and advertising prices.

Paperbacks

Paperback prices can be determined by a number of factors. For example, what kind of paperback are you going to illustrate? Historical romances with a guaranteed, built-in readership always have bigger cover art budgets than science fiction or gothic titles, which appeal to a much smaller audience.

Are you working on a "blockbuster" novel that the paperback house just paid ten million dollars for, or is the book cover you are illustrating a western with an audience of thirty-five lonely Texans and a horse? The art or photography budget will be affected by the reputation of the book and how many books the publisher thinks will be produced and sold. Economics play a very important part in the paperback and general book business.

Do you, as an artist or photographer, have a reputation in the paperback field for working in the right style with a good track record to match? There really are artists in the field whom art directors refer to as the "King of Romance" or the "King of Action." Their fees will be higher because their art can almost guarantee sales.

Is the illustration or photograph going to be used on the front cover only, or will it stretch over to the back of the book as well (called a "wrap")? Obviously, the "wrap" justifies more money than the single cover.

Do you work regularly with the paperback company? Are you doing a series for them or just a single title? For example, you might get $2,000 for a single job, but accept $1,700 for that same job if the cover is part of a series you will do.

And, finally, are you under contract to a paperback company for a certain number of books over the course of a contract covering a year or more? If you are, then your per-cover price might be lower than your individual price because you are guaranteed a year's work by that paperback company. Contracts usually mean that you are precluded from working with any other paperback company during the life of the contract. You can, however, do advertising or movie or other noncompetitive jobs at the same time. Recently, there has been a trend toward nonexclusive contracts that permit the illustrator to work for other paperback companies at the same time, as long as the other books do not contain the same subject matter. A nonexclusive contract simply means that you will give precedence in time and schedule to the books from the paperback company that has you under contract.

All of these things can determine the price you will receive from a paperback company. If you are a new illustrator or photographer, you cannot expect to receive the same price as an established veteran. The longer you work in the paperback field, and the more successful you become, the bigger the prices you can quote and receive.

Photography prices in the paperback field are generally lower than advertising prices and are determined on a basis similar to that described above.

Movie Art and Photography Prices

Movies can mean big money or very little money. It depends upon the movie (unfortunately, not every movie is a *Star Wars*). Every artist or photographer starts with low-budget movies (just like actors and actresses) and dreams about the studio extravaganzas. It takes time to work your way up the ladder.

Regardless of what kind of movie you are working on, movie pricing usually consists of three distinct stages, and each stage should be negotiated separately:

The Finished Sketch Fee. This is a tight, black and white sketch and is used for presentation and concept purposes. Because several artists may be working on the same movie at the same time, the fee offered for this finished sketch could be quite low. However, if you have a good movie track record and are working on the movie alone, then it will be considerably higher.

You are entitled to be paid in full for your tight pencil sketch, regardless of whether your sketch is the winner or not.

The Finished Comp Fee. This is really a finished piece of art, done in color or black and white, depending upon the requirements of the client. The artwork may be needed specifically for a black and white newspaper campaign, or for a full-color poster only, or a combination of both. It is primarily used for presentation purposes, but sometimes ends up as the final piece of art.

Again, you will be paid in full for this finished piece of art even when it is not the final choice of the movie studio. Don't forget: yours may be one of many finished comps competing with one another.

The Finish Fee. The movie finish is the winning comp described above, which becomes the actual movie poster or newspaper advertising campaign. The illustrator will be paid an additional fee.

The money paid for using this finished piece of art could be substantial, depending upon the reputation of the artist and the importance of the movie.

Pricing for Additional Usage. If the finished art that you produced for that movie poster is going to be used in other ways besides movie advertising (for example, as program art in the theater, or on T-shirts), you are entitled to additional money, as long as you negotiated this up front. It is extremely important to get all movie conditions in writing, either in a purchase order or a letter.

Also, you should negotiate for the return of your artwork after it has been used. This should be discussed at the beginning of the project and included in the letter of agreement or purchase order.

Here is a hypothetical example of movie pricing at work which might clear up some confusion:

Finished sketch fee: $1,500. You will get paid that amount regardless of whether you are asked to go to a finished comp or not.

Finished comp fee: $3,000. This figure, obviously, could be much higher, but for purposes of this example, you and the client have agreed to this price. Again, you will be paid that amount regardless of whether the art is the "winner" or not.

So now you are up to a total price of $4,500.

The finish fee: $5,000. You've won, and the client is now going to pay you a finish price of $5,000 for using your art in the final movie advertising campaign. And remember: this additional $5,000 required no additional work on your part. However, if a change is required to the finished piece of art, this change is billable.

So now, your movie price has ballooned to $9,500.

Additional usage fee: The client wants to build a major new promotion around your art (twenty-million balloons, all with your art printed on them, dropped over Times Square during a police raid on a movie theater), so you must negotiate an additional fee for this special usage (if the client knew about this promotion at the onset, the terms should have been included in the initial purchase order). You now agree to an additional fee of $5,000 so he can use the art on this promotion, but you still get the art back.

Now your movie fee has increased to $14,500.

But hold the phone. The head of the movie studio has decided that your art would make the perfect backdrop to his Bel Air swimming pool, so he offers you another $3,000 to buy the art for this purpose. You make a counteroffer: a fee of $5,500, which will guarantee the studio head the right not only to hang the art on his wall, but also to use the art wherever or however he wants to use it. He agrees to this final and complete buy-out; so your final movie project is now worth an even $20,000.

But remember, you could have been cut off at any phase of the project, and, unfortunately, in the movie business, the number of close calls far outnumber the big money successes.

When pricing photography for movie advertising, the process is basically the same. However, instead of producing finished sketches, the photographer will shoot very "loose" concept photographs before proceeding with the actual shootings. These "loose" concept photographs are used in the same way as illustrated finished sketches and priced accordingly.

Annual Report Pricing

A photographer is hired on a shooting "day-rate" plus expenses when he or she is hired to shoot an annual report. A "day-rate" enables the client to obtain a variety of photographs to choose from, since it is often impossible to determine exactly what should be covered on location, or what should be included in the final annual report. The photographer should always specify the number of photographs to be sold to the client as a result of his day's shooting.

Annual report illustration pricing is determined on a per-page basis, with full color illustrations costing more than black and white illustrations. Usually, the client has some idea of what he wants to pay for illustration; however, this is an area for negotiation. Perhaps a "package" price will be agreed to, which will enable the client to acquire a greater number of illustrations at a reasonable price than if he bought each illustration separately.

SOME OTHER IMPORTANT PRICING AREAS

"Kill" Fees

Suppose a particular project is not used by the client in his advertisement, magazine, etc. What should the talent charge that is fair to all parties concerned? Most agents and professional organizations recommend the following guidelines:

- If the artist or photographer has completed the job to the satisfaction of all concerned, but either the client or the advertising agency has a last-minute change in marketing direction and cannot use the photograph or illustration, the talent is entitled to a full fee plus any expenses.

- If the job has not been completed, but a considerable amount of work has been done by the artist or photographer before the client terminates the project, the talent is entitled to 50 percent of the agreed-to price plus 100 percent of all expenses incurred up to that point.

- If the job is terminated at the sketch phase and no actual painting or shooting has been done, the talent is entitled to 25 percent of the agreed-to price plus 100 percent of all expenses incurred to date.

Although most reputable agents, as well as many clients, operate under the above guidelines, some clients may feel that "kill" fees are negotiable and may want to pay less than the guidelines specified above. If that is the case, the artist or photographer must determine whether the "kill" fee offered is acceptable.

Changes

Normally, an artist or photographer is entitled to charge for changes. However, there are certain guidelines which should be considered:

- If an illustrator turns in a painting and the client asks that a minor change be made, a change that will not materially affect the painting itself, this is considered a "free" one-time change.

- However, if an artist turns in a finished painting and the client wants the painting substantially altered, so that it is quite different from the originally approved sketch, then the illustrator is entitled to charge for that change. How much he charges is a negotiable item and might be based on the complexity of the change and how much time was spent in doing it.

- It is very important that each sketch be approved by the client before the artist proceeds with any painting whatsoever. That sketch will serve as the basis for any and all chargeable changes in the future.

Photography Reshoots

Here are the guidelines concerning photography reshoots:

- If the art director is at a shoot and approves what is being shot, and the photographer delivers film based on that approved shooting, the art director assumes the responsibility. A reshoot, if required, will be at the client's expense. However, if the photographer is negligent and fails, for example, to put film in his camera, or loses the finished prints, then obviously, the photographer is at fault and would have to assume the expenses of the reshoot.

- If the client changes direction and asks the photographer to reshoot an entirely new approach, even though the first approach was finished and accepted, the photographer is entitled to an additional, full reshooting fee plus all expenses. In effect, he will handle it as a new assignment.

- If the photographer and the client are on the photographer's set during a shoot, it is possible that the photographer will shoot the same set several different ways, under the direction of the client. If this takes place, the photographer should negotiate additional money for all additional shooting.

The Purchase Order

The importance of receiving a purchase order from a client, covering all illustration and photography work to be performed, cannot be over-emphasized. Once a price has been negotiated between the client and the talent, a purchase order spelling out the complete terms and conditions of the sale, including rights to be purchased, job restrictions, expenses to be covered, and, of course, price, should be prepared and issued to the illustrator and photographer. This purchase order will help both the client and the talent understand exactly what was bought and sold, and should prevent future problems.

But suppose a client does not issue a purchase order until after the job has been completed. In that case, the purchase order should be issued as a confirmation of the work done. If you are unable to obtain a purchase order prior to starting a job, it is wise to at least send a letter to the art director, outlining the complete terms of the agreement. The art director can then refer to that letter as the basis for a confirming purchase order.

SOME OTHER KEY QUESTIONS ABOUT PRICING

Suppose an illustrator or photographer underprices a job unintentionally? Is he or she committed to that price? The answer is "yes." However, if a talent seriously underprices a job — it does happen — the talent should approach the art director on a one-to-one basis and honestly explain the problem. In most cases, a reasonable art director will allow the talent to renegotiate the price. However, the art director is under no obligation to do so. If the art director has already issued a purchase order to the talent, spelling out the "underprice," then there is very little anyone can do, and the talent must make the best of a difficult situation.

Must an illustrator or photographer always give the art director a price "on-the-spot?"

If a talent is in doubt about what price to charge, it is best to tell the art director that you would like to check out several factors in order to give him the fairest price possible. The illustrator or photographer should then check out the industry guide-lines, perhaps call a few artist or photographer friends for their comments, and figure out exactly how long the job will take, and what special cost problems might be involved. In other words, you, the artist, must come up with a knowledgeable price based on as many facts as can be obtained, not just a price "out of your head." You should not cheat the client, but you should also not cheat yourself. No client will ever object to receiving a carefully thought out and reasonable price, based on research and experience.

In the case of photography, it is essential to cost out models, props, special location conditions, hair and make-up costs, and many other potential expenses before giving any price to the art director. Continual miscalculations on expenses can put a photographer out of business quickly.

Good expense records are vital because an illustrator or photographer will not be reimbursed for any expenses unless expense receipts in writing are submitted to the client.

A WORD ABOUT COPYRIGHT AND REPRODUCTION RIGHTS

This subject is probably the most confusing to all artists and photographers, and yet is extremely significant in terms of the final and fair negotiation of a price.

Under the new copyright law of 1978, the copyright belongs to the artist or photographer — the originator of the art or photograph — and can only be transferred in writing. In other words, the artist or photographer must literally sign away the copyright to another party.

Reproduction rights can be sold by the artist and photographer as many times as he wishes, depending upon what is negotiated with the client.

If first reproduction rights are sold, then the purchaser can use the photograph or painting once for a very specific purpose. If the client wants to use that photograph or illustration in other areas, or reproduce it a second, third, or more times, additional fees must be paid for these uses. The client is not free to use the art or photograph wherever he chooses.

If all reproduction rights are sold, the client has bought just that: all rights to reproduce the painting or photograph wherever he wants. Physical ownership of the painting or photograph, however, should be part of the negotiation. Sometimes, the painting or photograph is sold to the client and the client retains physical possession of the painting or photograph. Other times, the painting or photograph is returned to the talent and remains in the talent's possession.

When the client buys all reproduction rights and also retains possession of the painting or photograph, the client has effected what is called a "buy-out."

WORK FOR HIRE

The "work for hire" phrase simply means that the painting or photograph has been produced as if the artist or photographer were an employee of the client's corporation. In essence, the copyright and authorship of the painting or photograph is owned by the client's corporation and not by the artist or photographer. The Supreme Court has finally ruled that the rights to any artwork belong completely to the free-lance artist and no "work for hire" or other transfer of rights can be made unless the artist agrees to transfer those rights in writing. This decision was due, in large part, to the long and persistent efforts of every single professional organization in the field, and must be applauded by every free-lancer.

For in-depth discussion of copyright and work for hire, you can consult *Legal Guide for the Visual Artist* by Tad Crawford (Allworth Press, distributed by North Light Books, 1-800-289-0963).

SUMMARY

The real value of any painting or photograph lies in its reproduction rights. If a client buys all reproduction rights, and the artist or photographer retains physical ownership of the piece, the artist or photographer has really sold all that is valuable in that painting or photograph. The artist or photographer simply owns the work plus very limited usage (personal use, exhibition purposes, etc.). While an artist or photographer may want to retain physical ownership of his or her painting or photograph, it is actually the reproduction rights of that painting or photograph that are marketable (if you are in the company of a Norman Rockwell or an Edward Steichen, then your original painting or photograph would have great value).

It cannot be stressed too strongly that the artist or photographer must always negotiate what he or she is selling before the job is accepted. The talent should know exactly what is being sold: first-time rights, all reproduction rights, all rights including copyright and ownership. These different situations should be priced accordingly and should be negotiated and agreed to before any job is accepted.

All of the many aspects concerning the selling of rights, copyright, etc., should be studied carefully by the artist or photographer before entering the marketplace. In particularly complicated negotiations, the artist or photographer may want to consult with an attorney versed in the intricacies of the graphic arts field. The chapters of the local Graphic Artists Guild, ASMP, or APA may be of some help in this particular area, especially since they may have listings of attorneys who are experienced in copyright law. The Volunteer Lawyers for the Arts might also be helpful and may have a volunteer group near you.

Usually clients want either first reproduction rights or a specified number of rights. In advertising, clients usually want to own the art or photograph. When this is the case, this condition is usually spelled out by the agency beforehand, and the price reflects this.

Broadly speaking, in editorial markets, the reproduction rights are more limited, and the artist or photographer usually retains ownership of the work. There are, however, exceptions to this rule and there are legal proceedings in progress that may change certain procedures. The best rule to follow is: Negotiate every job before accepting it and spell out exactly what is being bought and sold.

Minding Your Business

Some Important Business Aspects of Commercial Art and Photography You Should Know

As an artist or photographer in business for yourself you will have to decide, at some point, what form your free-lance business will take.

The three forms usually considered are the sole proprietorship, the partnership, and the corporation. Before taking any steps at all, you should first discuss your personal business situation with your accountant and your lawyer. They can best advise you as to which form of business would be appropriate for you. The views expressed in this section are simply here to get you thinking about the various forms your business might take and some of the advantages and disadvantages of each. Again, no business decision should be made by you until you have consulted with your attorney or accountant.

THE CORPORATION

Essentially there are two forms of corporations. There is the regular or "C" corporation, and there is the subchapter "S" corporation. The "C" or regular corporation is the one most familiar to all of us. The regular corporation can be something as large as General Motors or as small as a design studio with two people who simply choose to incorporate themselves into a "C" or regular corporation.

Here are some of the benefits of *any* corporation that should be mentioned:

- A corporation has limited liability, and, as an employee of the corporation, you also have limited liability. This means that shareholders, officers, and directors are not liable for the debts of a corporation, and the corporation is liable only to the extent that it has assets.

- If a corporation wishes to raise capital, it can issue shares of stock based on the amount of capital that any given person wishes to invest in the corporation.

- You can distribute shares of the corporation to your family. In the realm of estate planning, this can be quite helpful.

- A corporation can be continued even if the key participant should die. All the monies are not tied up in estate or probate courts.

- A corporation can have profit-sharing programs (when your corporation has a surplus), and deferred compensation programs.

- All of these options can offer you a great deal of tax flexibility, and you should discuss the merits of incorporating with an expert in corporate accounting and law.

Disadvantages include:

- The big disadvantage is that it costs money to set up the corporation. Although there are many books advising you on how to incorporate yourself, you should really hire an attorney to set up your corporation.

- In some states, you must pay a corporation tax even when your corporation operates at a loss.

- There is also a lot of paperwork involved. Aside from the federal, state, and, sometimes, city tax forms, you must file workmen's compensation, unemployment compensation, social security, and your corporate pension tax papers if you have a corporate pension program. You will also have to keep minutes of your stockholder meetings, which means more paperwork for you.

- Also, some people feel that your chances of being audited are greater with a corporation than with an individual filing a return. However, as your income keeps rising, your prospects of being audited by the IRS are going to be reasonably good anyway. If your corporate pension program grows to any sizable amount, the IRS will also keep an close eye on how the trustees (probably yourself) are administering those assets. However, if the tax advantages for you are sizable, you may find that this is a small price to pay for the savings earned.

The Sub-Chapter "S" Corporation

The sub-chapter "S" corporation is similar to a regular or "C" corporation except that it is taxed like a partnership. Shareholders of the "S" corporation can take advantage of all of the retirement benefits that the "C" or regular corporation offers, but, unlike the "C" corporation, the losses from the sub-chapter "S" corporation can be taken on the individual shareholder's tax return and losses that cannot be taken in a specific year can be carried to a year when they can be used. And unlike a "C" corporation where income can be taxed twice (since dividends from a corporation can also be taxed), the income from an "S" corporation is only taxed once. Obviously free-lancers looking into incorporation should carefully check the benefits of the "C" versus the "S" form of incorporation with their accountant to see which form is of the most benefit to them.

PARTNERSHIPS AND SOLE PROPRIETORSHIPS

Probably one of the biggest advantages of sole proprietorships and partnerships, as compared to corporations, is that it costs less money to set up a partnership or a sole proprietorship. There is less record-keeping. You deduct the losses that might be incurred during the early life of the business from your personal return. Unlike corporate dividends, profits in a partnership are not subject to a second Federal income tax when distributed.

The disadvantages are as follows:

- Your unlimited; yes, unlimited liability.
- In a partnership, each member can bind the other members, so that one partner can cause the other individuals to be personally liable for any losses.
- Also, all profits are personally taxable to the owner (this is true of both a sole proprietorship and a partnership).
- As an owner in a partnership or sole proprietorship, you may not have full tax benefits from generous pension, profit-sharing, health, and other programs that could be set up by a corporation.

OTHER KEY BUSINESS CONSIDERATIONS

How Much Overhead Do You Need?

Since one is never sure what direction a business will take, the cardinal rule for the starting free-lancer is "keep the overhead low."

With the exception of the commercial photographer who has to make an investment in equipment (and even a small amount of photographic equipment can represent a king's ransom), most free-lancers will find they can dispense with expensive office space, secretaries, engraved stationery, etc.

In large metropolitan areas, it is quite possible to share space with other free-lancers. An illustrator also has the option of working out of his home. Even photographers will find that they can readily rent studio space or photographic equipment, and can use free-lance assistants and stylists.

A phone, an answering service (or a telephone-answering machine), and a fax machine are the other prerequisites. Get your portfolio shot on transparencies, those tearsheets laminated, your mailing piece printed, and you are ready to go.

What about Record Keeping?

After setting up the office, the next order of business is to get yourself an accountant. He will tell you what your liabilities are for sales taxes — when you have to collect them, where to file, and what other taxes you are liable for and when they should be paid. Be sure to check all of this out before you get too far into business. THIS IS VERY IMPORTANT. There are all too many situations when free-lancers are wiped out totally because they didn't know that they were liable for sales and other taxes and consequently never bothered to collect them. A discussion with your accountant on taxes before you go into business can save you a lot of money and grief in the long run.

Do You Need Office Help?

There are some excellent temporary services that will send you a secretary, a bookkeeper, a receptionist, etc., for the day you need them. You pay only for the time you use them. The agency pays all the taxes and overhead costs.

You can also farm out some of your "overload" to other free-lancers. You pay them a fee, but they pay their own taxes. In effect, they are free-lancers working with you, but not employees working for you. That is a very important distinction. If they are employees, you are liable for withholding taxes plus paying all corporate benefits. If you pay free-lancers more than $600 in one year, your accountant must file a 1099 on their earnings. But they will pay their own taxes and will not be part of your overhead.

What about Billing and Collecting?

Slow-paying clients represent one of the major complaints of all free-lancers. The slow-payer is bad enough, but the nonpayer is the real culprit.

Unfortunately, there are deadbeats in any business, and the free-lance business is no exception. There is only one piece of advice that makes any sense when it comes to people who do not pay their bills: DO NOT WORK WITH THEM. Let's face it. If no one would work with these kind of "clients," they would either go out of business, or mend their ways.

If potential clients call who are not major magazines, advertising agencies, or companies, you should check them out before working with them. Never let the prospective client know that you are checking it out, but, instead, call your fellow artists, other clients, or anyone who has worked with this prospective new account. Ask about the prospect's bill paying record. How long did the client take to pay? What kind of people were they to work with? If you get a lot of negative feedback, back away. DO NOT WORK WITH THAT CLIENT!

If everyone took this simple precaution at the beginning of a possible assignment, the no-pay client would merely be a bad memory.

The late payers are a different breed. Unfortunately, even some of the bluest of the blue chip accounts in town can be the slowest payers in the world. Since they are good for the money, and every free-lancer desperately wants to work for them, you must accept their late payments as one of the costs of doing business with them. Often these late-payers are investing their cash-flow in other ways. In the case of advertising agencies, they may be doing business with slow-paying clients of their own.

If you know that the client is a slow-payer and you have a lot of "clout" (you are a name talent), then you can specify, at the time you take the job, that you will only take the job if you either get some "up-front" money, or get paid in a specific period of time. Unfortunately, very few free-lancers have this kind of power.

As mentioned above, you can ask for an advance, which is a cash payment paid to you at the start of a project and deducted from the final bill. This is a commonplace occurrence among photographers since they often spend their own money to set up a shot, and the client has no difficulty in justifying advance money. It is less common in illustration (with the exception of advance travel funds), but there is no reason why an advance cannot be requested. The illustrator has to eat, too.

Another possibility, especially in the case of an on-going project (annual report, a series of brochures, an advertising campaign, or any project that will be spread over a period of a few months), is to bill in stages. For example, you could bill one-third up front, one-third in the middle of the job, and the balance at the completion of the job. Printers and other suppliers do this all the time. You would not do this for a $1,000 job that takes two weeks to complete, but you can do it for a $10,000 job that will keep you tied up for a period of time. Billing in stages will enable you to keep your cash flow at a very healthy level.

Sometimes a client will not give you an advance or allow you to bill in stages and, instead, will tell you at the beginning of the job: "I take 120 days to pay. Take it or leave it." That's the time when you ask yourself: "Do I really need that job?"

Suppose you are not sure of your new client's payment schedule, but thirty days have elapsed and nothing has come in the mail. You might consider sending another invoice just as a reminder. Invoices have been known to get misplaced or even lost. After about sixty days, send a copy of your invoice with a note asking if the bill, by any chance, was lost. Don't come on too strong because there may be a very legitimate reason why you have not received payment. The company may be on a sixty day payment schedule, and everything really is locked in the computer.

If the invoice is extremely late — ninety days or more — then a call to the art director or the accounting office is in order. Ask if there is any problem with your invoice. Sometimes verification of expenses can tie up a bill, and that may be a perfectly legitimate reason. Often, the art director has very little to do with processing invoices and once he approves payment, scheduling is out of his hands.

In large agencies, even the accounting office is powerless, since the mighty computer may have been programmed to make your payment on the 10th or the 26th of the month. If your invoice missed those two days, it will slip over to the next billing cycle.

There is not much you can do when it comes to these late-payment situations. You can try charging interest on your invoices, but unless a client has actually signed an agreement with you to pay interest on delinquent accounts, you have absolutely no way to enforce it.

Some photographers will discount an invoice two percent if it is paid in ten days, and sometimes this works. However, there have been cases where a client waited sixty days to pay and still took the two percent discount. Late payers are literally like the weather; everyone talks about them but no one seems to know what to do about them. Just when you think you have a client's payment schedule figured out, it changes and you are back to square one.

Let's get back, for the moment, to the client who doesn't pay at all. You should have known better, but you didn't. You took a job with someone you've never worked with before, no one could give you any information about them, and months have passed with apparently no prospect of payment. What do you do?

Well, you could hand it over to a collection agency which may or may not collect, but, if they are successful, their fees can range as high as 50 percent of the bill.

You could pay a lawyer to send a lawyer's letter, but that will cost you anywhere from $50 to $200 with no guarantee that it will work.

If the amount due you is small (less than a few thousand dollars), you could take the account to small claims court. Call the city clerk in your city. The issuing of a summons can usually be handled by mail. This official notice to appear in court is often enough to get fast action from your debtor.

Any kind of legal action can be expensive and there are numerous cases where an artist or photographer won the case, but lost the fee to the lawyer. Lawyers have to live, too, and legal action should always be a last resort. Instead, check out your clients much more carefully at the beginning, and you will end up with a much happier ending.

As you continue working in the freelance field, you will discover that you have some very good clients who take their time paying, and other very good clients who pay promptly. If you can get a diversity of clientele, it won't matter as much, since you will have a healthy cash flow and be able to meet your obligations without great difficulty. This is really what good business is all about. That's a good reason to avoid the single client situation, because if that client happens to be a slow-payer, you will probably find yourself in a feast-or-famine situation.

BUSINESS CHECKLIST

You are in business for yourself and your business judgment will affect your profitability.

• Set up the most efficient and effective business organization for yourself; i.e., a corporation, sole proprietorship, or partnership. Your lawyer is your best friend.

• Keep your overhead low. Compare prices from time to time on all supplies and services you buy.

• Get an accountant. Keep accurate records. Keep a close watch on how much your business is taking in and how much money you are paying out. Know at all times how much you owe and how much is owed to you.

• Pay your taxes — all your taxes — on time. The government is not a patient creditor.

• Check out all questionable clients and don't work for the "deadbeats." Bill promptly and set up your collection procedures efficiently. Work for a diversity of clients to insure a good, steady cash-flow. Keep your borrowing to a minimum, and repay loans promptly. Your credit rating is important.

• Look ahead, plan ahead; for the next year, for five years from now.

• Take an inventory of your assets at least twice a year, so you won't suddenly be caught short of important supplies, tools, or equipment.

• Finally, preserve, at all costs, your reputation for being a competent and honest businessman. The right business reputation will ultimately mean the difference between success and failure.

The Artist and Photographer Representative

6

At some point in his or her career, the artist or photographer usually asks: Do I need someone to represent me in the marketplace? The answer can be critical to any career.

Unless you are particularly good at marketing your own work, a good representative (also called an agent) can be a definite asset. Notice that the emphasis is on the word "good," because a bad agent is worse than no agent at all.

Where and how do you find a good representative? There is an organization called SPAR — The Society of Photographers and Artists Representatives — and you can obtain a listing of their members by writing to them at the address included in the Addendum of this book. This listing will include the top agents in the commercial art and photography field, with a heavy emphasis on the New York area, since most major agents operate in New York. The SPAR membership listing breaks down the representatives by the general categories of illustration and photography, and, specifically, the kind of illustration and photography handled (still life, fashion, photorealism, etc.). Although the SPAR membership list is a good place to start in your search for an agent, the list does not outline specifically how each agent works, or the kind of talent he or she is looking for at a particular time. Consequently, you should send a sample of your work (a black and white Xerox will do just fine) to all those agents who handle illustration, photography, or both and follow up on any response you get. A telephone call to the agent before a mailing piece is sent out will waste your time and the agent's.

If you don't like the "blind" approach mentioned above, you should consider calling several art directors directly and asking them whom they would recommend. If the same names keep coming up (and they usually do), contact these agents through your direct mailing piece. After all, the art director is the person that the representative is dealing with, and, if he thinks the agent is doing a good job selling him, chances are the agent will do a good job representing you.

Usually, the worst source of information about agents is other artists or photographers, because they are often reluctant to "share" their agent with possible competitors. It's like the person who finds that great little French restaurant and is afraid to make it too popular. The art director, however, has no personal involvement and will judge the agent purely on his or her professional merits, which should be your prime consideration as well.

FINDING AND INTERVIEWING THE AGENT

Let's say you've located several agents, and two of them are very interested in you. Which one do you choose? This is, obviously, a very personal decision. You have to like and respect the person who will be your representative. Also, you have to be in agreement about philosophy and goals.

Is the agent as promotion- and publicity-minded as you are?

Is the agent interested in monetary goals alone and is that really your main consideration?

Is the agent interested in balancing and building your career for the future instead of just a short-term "one-job-at-a-time" relationship?

And what about your goals? Do you primarily want income, regardless of the circumstances?

Or are you primarily interested in recognition, with money taking a distant second place?

Or are you mainly concerned with the jobs that give you artistic satisfaction, and really don't care about national recognition or money?

The list of goals and aspirations is endless, but, in any event, you and your agent must be in general agreement. That is why you should take as much time as necessary interviewing agents, asking them about their market philosophy, getting to know the kind of work done by the other talent the agents represent, and getting as much information as possible before making a decision. Any ethical agent will appreciate your taking the time to make an informed decision. An agent/talent relationship is like a marriage. It should be a long-term commitment and not be entered into hastily.

WHAT DOES AN AGENT DO?

In the ideal relationship, the agent is the marketing and selling arm of the talent. The agent "packages" your product (art or photography) by getting your portfolio in selling condition and ready for business. The agent takes your product to market by showing it to all possible prospective customers. The agent promotes and advertises your product and does everything possible to enhance your career.

On the practical side, the agent usually plans and sets up advertising and direct mail campaigns, negotiates all prices and what those prices include (reproduction rights, buy-outs, etc.), does the billing and collecting of all fees, handles the collection of all sales taxes, develops all publicity programs for the talent, handles agency shows and presentations, opens new accounts and markets, and expands existing markets.

What the agent does not do is act as your researcher, stylist, typist, or social director. The agent is your marketing arm; the person who is in tune with you and your aspirations, sells your talent, and helps build your career.

HOW IS THE AGENT COMPENSATED?

Normally, the agent works on a commission basis of 25 percent of all local business, whether acquired by the agent or the talent. On out-of-town accounts, the commission is usually 30 percent, since the agent's selling and servicing expenses (air freight, long-distance telephone calls, trips when required) are higher. Also, if an agent represents out-of-town artists or photographers, the 30 percent commission applies.

This 25 percent commission on all local business and 30 percent on all out-of-town business is the basis used by the majority of "name" agents. However, there are some other considerations that should be mentioned.

Some photographers with large billings will hire an agent on salary. The photographer will cover all the expenses of the agent's business (such as telephone, entertainment, etc.) and may even offer a small commission on all business in addition to salary. However, the agent is a paid employee of the photographer and is not a "free agent." Normally, an illustrator cannot afford a full-time employee because, unlike a photographer, the illustrator is seldom capable of generating a large volume of business on a consistent basis.

Another financial compensation arrangement that is growing in use, primarily in the photography area, is the one in which the agent receives a standard 25 percent commission on all print photographs, but becomes a 50 percent partner with the photographer when television production work is involved. For example, the agent and the photographer will set up a television production corporation in which both will have 50 percent of the stock. Both will share equally in the profits of the corporation and the expenses of the corporation. This television production corporation is entirely separate from the agent's and the photographer's regular corporations.

In another arrangement,the agent agrees to become a personal business manager to the artist or photographer and will receive a fee of 35 to 50 percent of all billings. A personal manager will become much more involved with the talent's career than simply marketing his product. Because of the intensive involvement, such a personal manager can only represent one or two talents. The range of personal services might include investment counseling, setting up and maintaining pension programs, even utilizing a power of attorney to pay bills and taxes, etc. This personal attention to a talent's total career commands, for the personal agent/manager, a larger commission on all billings.

There is also the "broker" arrangement where an agent can represent an artist or photographer in one or two specific areas, but not in all markets, or may take a commission (normally 25 percent) only on work that the agent brings into the studio. Under this plan, there is almost no commitment to the talent on the part of the agent, since the agent is not responsible for the talent's career or growth, but only for that work which he himself sells. The agent cannot be responsible for more because the bulk of the talent's business may be in what is referred to in the industry as "house accounts". A house account is one that the artist or photographer controls completely. He sells it. Services it. Handles all complaints. Does the billing on it. Is completely responsible for it. The artist or photographer does not pay a commission to anyone on a house account.

Because brokers do not share in the total business of an artist or photographer, these agents must "load up" with a great number of artists or photographers to offset the money lost by not being able to take a full twenty-five percent commission on all work handled by a talent. Obviously, if a "broker" can get one job a year for fifty different artists, his profits can be substantial.

Most serious and dedicated agents believe that the broker arrangement is not as professional as the "full 25 percent" or exclusive representation arrangement. However, there are artists and photographers who want to maintain their own house accounts and feel that any business a broker brings in is added business at a minimum cost.

BILLING AND PAYMENT PROCEDURES

Usually, the agent does all the billing of jobs and the collecting of all fees, as well as the collecting of all sales taxes. This is becoming an important part of the collecting process because state sales tax departments are increasing their surveillance of all firms.

The billing procedure is quite simple. When the check from the client arrives, the agent takes his 25 percent commission, as well as any sales tax owed, and forwards the difference, plus any reimburseable expenses, to the artist or photographer. Because the agent has already forwarded either a copy of the purchase order or his invoice, or both, to the artist when the job was billed, the artist can now compare what he is receiving to what was on the original invoice and can reconcile the payment.

Every artist or photographer should insist that the agent doing the billing follow this procedure. Since there is not an employee/employer relationship between the artist and the agent, no income tax is withheld. At the end of the year, the agent's accountant will send a Form 1099 to the artist, which contains the amount of income earned by the artist during a calendar year. Both the talent and the agent pay their own social security and withholding taxes.

In the case of photography (and also in illustration when applicable), the agent takes his or her commission after all expenses have been deducted from the gross bill. Oftentimes, a photographer will incur many expenses such as models and stylists, and the check issued by the client to the agent includes reimbursement for these expenses. The agent is not entitled to commission on these expenses, only on the shooting fee.

WHAT ABOUT EXPENSES?

The artist and photographer cover all of their own expenses: studio rental, telephone, art supplies, messengers.

The agent covers all of his or her expenses: office, travel, telephone, entertainment. When billable expenses are involved (models, hairdressers, etc.), and there is no advance from the client to cover these expenses, the artist or photographer covers the cost. The agent adds them to the final invoice.

If the agent needs more transparencies for the portfolio or wants a tear sheet laminated, the artist or photographer will pay for this, since, ultimately, the portfolio belongs to the talent.

However, if a client in a faraway city wants to see a portfolio, the cost of air freighting the portfolio is absorbed by the agent, since this is considered a selling expense. Figuring out who pays for what usually takes plain common sense, but it is a good idea to spell it out formally.

As far as promotional expenses are concerned, the agent and the talent usually split the cost of printing and mailing or advertising on a 75 percent talent/25 percent agent basis. The rationale: the sharing of expenses should be the same ratio as the sharing of profits. Before any relationship between an artist or photographer and an agent is consummated, all of these financial "splits" should be fully discussed and agreed to, so that both parties clearly understand the terms of the arrangement.

WHO DOESN'T NEED AN AGENT?

First of all, there are some artists or photographers who genuinely like to sell their own work to clients and are extraordinarily adept at it. They like to negotiate prices, to overcome objections, to present their own work the way they think it should be presented. These artists and photographers have the capacity not only to do the work but to sell it as well. It would probably be a mistake for people like this to get involved with an agent.

Then there are those talents who want to work only for certain segments of the market (limited editorial, children's books, etc.), or talents who are interested in making a moderate income and are not interested in doing every job that comes along. Unfortunately, their more relaxed life-style and way of doing business takes money away from the agent and it is better if the artist or photographer represents himself.

Also, there are artists who are in offbeat areas, such as soft sculpture, wallpaper designs, or crafts, whose market areas do not justify having an agent. Most agents deal through advertising agencies, paperback houses, movie studios, and major publishing accounts. Artists in other areas can better represent themselves. The same is true of talents who work in the fine art fields.

In general, there are just too few agents for the number of artists and photographers desiring representation. If you exclude agents who represent retouchers and printers, there are only a few hundred qualified artist and photographer representatives in the entire country. Yet there are probably thousands of artists and photographers looking for representation. Among the established agents, half represent photographers only, another group handles television, and the third group specializes in particular market areas, such as fashion or publishing. The odds of a general illustrator finding a good agent may be difficult indeed. This is why so many free-lancers end up representing themselves.

THE IMPORTANCE OF THE AGENT/TALENT CONTRACT

Many agent/talent relationships exist merely on the basis of a handshake or a verbal agreement, yet they can last a lifetime.

At the other end of the scale are the iron-clad, thoroughly documented, legally correct documents that spell out, detail by detail, who does what in the relationship.

And then there is the middle-ground agreement or contract that outlines generally who is responsible for what without covering all specific items in detail.

The important thing to remember is that a contract is only as good as the parties who sign it. There is no contract in existence today that cannot be broken or abrogated if one or the other party wants to do it. A contract really should be an affirmation of trust between two working parties. Nothing more. Nothing less. If mutual respect between two parties breaks down, a contract will only serve as the basis for lengthy and often bitter litigation from which no one gains except the lawyers.

Most professional organizations recommend some kind of contract or written agreement between an agent and a talent. A contract can make things easier when misunderstandings arise. It can spell out the responsibilities of each party regarding expenses and duties. And the contract can detail the termination agreement. There is a generally acknowledged standard in the graphic arts industry supported by the Joint Ethics Committee (JEC) that, in the event of a termination between an agent and the talent, the agent is entitled to six months commission on accounts after the date of termination. SPAR recommends that their members increase this time of compensation by one month for every year of the relationship. Thus, if a photographer and agent split after ten years, the agent would receive commissions for sixteen months instead of six months. This principle, by the way, has been upheld in several legal decisions over the past few years.

This stipulation is put in contracts to protect an agent who might work on an account for months and even years, only to see that account come to fruition after the agent and the talent have terminated their relationship.

Or, an agent may have developed a client that assures a photographer or artist years of income. Surely, the agent is entitled to more than the one-time immediate commission for that job.

Normally, when an agent and talent sever a relationship, the agent will submit in writing those accounts, both present and future, where business has been written and a commission is due the agent, or where future business will be written in all probability during the next six months. Obviously, the agent cannot submit the entire art director's list of every large agency and say he or she is entitled to all business coming through that agency. The account list should be honest, carefully constructed, and reasonable. All business generated through these specific accounts during the next six months mean a commission for the agent.

In mutually agreeable terminations (and there really are some like that), there is usually no problem with future agent compensation. Still, a written contract or letter of agreement can help avoid any misunderstanding.

KEY QUESTIONS TO ASK AGENTS

Do the agents...

- Represent only artists and photographers that they believe in and are they totally committed to them?
- Believe in being more than agents and becoming involved in the total career of the artists they represent?
- Appreciate the problems of the artist and try, whenever possible, to alleviate these problems?
- Also appreciate the problems of the art director; his client/agency relationship, tight deadlines, and budget limitations; and try to help him solve these problems whenever they can?
- Believe in full representation? That means taking on only that number of artists that they can fully represent as well as insuring that each artist is noncompetitive in style with other artists they represent?
- Believe in giving full service to their artists and to the art director, promptly and professionally? Every client, no matter what the job price, deserves the very best the agents and the artists can offer.
- Believe in being flexible? Business conditions change. The economy rises and falls. Accounts switch. Agents and artists must adjust to all changes in order to survive successfully.
- Believe in always meeting deadlines and always keeping a bargain? Agents and artists are only as good as their word and their last job.
- Believe in being honest at all times? With their artists? With the art director? With themselves?
- Believe in their profession, the profession of representing artists, and believe that theirs is truly the most exciting and challenging profession anywhere. Are they proud to be a part of it?

Opportunities for the Free-Lance, Out-of-Town Artist and Photographer

7

Many artists and photographers in this country make good, even incredible incomes, working within a one-hundred-mile radius of their homes. Why is it, then, that so many of them hunger for the big, metropolitan markets, especially the biggest market of them all: New York. An artist or photographer may be recognized throughout Europe, or be a celebrity in the art world in other areas of this country, but making it in the "Big Apple" remains his life-long goal.

Other people are just looking for markets to supplement their local income, and New York is just as good a place to do that as any other.

And then, some artists and photographers, although happy with the money they are making in their local area, are unhappy with the lack of diversity in the kinds of jobs they are forced to deal with on a day-to-day basis; so they, too, want the creative challenge of New York. They need New York with its many magazines, publishing houses, and diversity of advertising agencies and accounts.

Finally, some just want to be part of one of the largest creative communities in the world — from the groups of fine artists living in SoHo, to the large number of big-name, and not-so-big-name illustrators living in nearby Connecticut, to the hundreds of photographers working in studios throughout midtown Manhattan.

And New York is not only the largest market for illustrators and photographers, but also the most innovative and progressive in many other areas.

For example, the Society of Illustrators, the Graphic Artists Guild, the American Society of Magazine Photographers and the American Institute of Graphic Arts, to name just a few, all headquarter in New York.

Name any superstar of international consequence and chances are he or she will have top representation in New York.

The greatest number of representatives handling the largest contingent of both artists and photographers have offices in New York.

Most of the movements in the free-lance field, such as the fight for fees on reproduction rights, started through professional organizations in New York.

So, to lots of people, New York is the place where the action starts, where they can meet and interact with their peers, where getting the respect of their peers is something that no one can put a price on.

The ideal to many artists and photographers, of course, is to live in New Orleans or Cape Cod or Denver and still tap the New York market. That is obviously the best of both worlds. You do those jobs locally that appeal to you and "pay the rent," and yet you have access to the "big money" and "big-time" jobs in New York. Occasionally, a client will pay your way to New York on assignment, so there's even the possibility of a partially paid vacation in the deal.

When most artists or photographers think "out-of-town," New York is the first city that comes to mind. But if you are going to think "out-of-town" seriously, then think of other cities. Strangely enough, those who work in the New York market aggressively seek out work in Chicago, Boston, Dallas, Houston, Los Angeles, Atlanta, and Detroit, to name a few. Some of the best jobs and best customers are outside New York. Many New York-based representatives, artists, and photographers get one-third or more of their business from accounts outside the New York area.

Clients in Chicago or Los Angeles are used to dealing with New York talent, and these clients are accustomed to making provisions for the extra time involved in working with out-of-town talent. So if you, the freelancer, are thinking of seriously expanding your markets, don't just think in terms of New York. Aim for every major metropolitan market. You may find that one of these markets will give you more work than you can handle, and you will not need New York at all. Or you may be lucky and proficient enough to work in all major markets, including New York, and have the best of all worlds.

Now, the big question for the out-of-town illustrator and photographer is: Can it be done? What, realistically, are your chances of reaching beyond your own local marketing area and grabbing those big national jobs? How difficult is it to sell yourself in big markets like New York, when the competition is overwhelming? What do you need to crack the large markets, and what are the pitfalls to avoid in trying to crash these areas, so that you are not completely destroyed in the process?

To put it bluntly, it is not easy for the illustrator or photographer living in Des Moines or Waco or Butte to compete aggressively and successfully in the big metropolitan markets, but it can be done. However, there are certain guidelines that should be considered:

If possible, get yourself an agent to handle your work in these metropolitan areas. Unfortunately, that is easier said than done. A good agent can act as your eyes and ears in these markets. He or she serves as your presence. The client who is buying the art or photography knows who to contact if a portfolio must be seen, or a price must be quoted, or a problem arises. A good agent can continually promote you and show your work around town. If you are a thousand miles away from where the action is, obviously, you cannot react instantly to what is "happening" on the street. An agent can, and, suddenly, your being out-of-town isn't quite the disaster the art director thought it would be.

But getting a good agent (and that's the only kind to get — you are better off with no agent than a bad agent) can be difficult. Many agents, quite frankly, do not want to handle out-of-town talent. It costs more. There is more room for things to go wrong (that guaranteed overnight freight service that sounds so great in the advertisements suddenly doesn't look so great when your finish is two days late or, worst of all, lost or damaged). Yet all agents are interested in making money and filling a market need, and if you are doing something that is truly saleable in big markets, an agent will probably be interested in you.

How do you find an agent who might be interested in out-of-town talent?

The first thing to do is get the SPAR (Society of Photographers and Artists Representatives) list of agents. This list shows the talent each agent represents. You will probably recognize the names of certain illustrators and photographers who live outside New York or Chicago or other large areas. That could be a tip-off that the agent is not afraid of out-of-town talent and may even be encouraging them. Drop a mailing piece showing your style to those agents who might be good possibilities, and then follow up with a phone call. If an agent is interested in what you are doing, eventually you should meet face-to-face and begin planning how you and the agent will tap these major markets.

But suppose you cannot get an agent to represent you — or perhaps you don't want an agent at all (you may not want to pay the 30 to 35 percent commission off the top that most good agents will ask for when handling out-of-town talent, as compared to the standard 25 percent you would pay in-town). Then you should be aware of certain realities that exist concerning the out-of-town free-lancer:

REALITIES OF BIG CITY MARKETS FOR THE OUT-OF-TOWN FREE-LANCER

It is easier to be an out-of-town illustrator than an out-of-town photographer. Let's face it. As long as the illustrator gets his work in on time, there is little need for the art director to have any face-to-face dealings with the artist. Most details can be handled by telephone or a sketch or even a letter.

But compare that situation with a photographer who must constantly deal with a client, both before, during, and after a shooting; it makes no difference what kind of photography he is doing (still-life, industrial, people, etc.), or whether the photographer has an in-town agent or not. Ever try to get an array of beautiful models of all shapes and sizes outside New York, when all the major modelling agencies have their headquarters in New York? Not easy to do. And multiply that by almost any other kind of service (more printers, retouchers, stylists, photo equipment outlets, etc.), and you can see the problems that an out-of-town photographer faces.

On the other hand, if you, as a photographer, have excellent studio space outside New York that can be used for special shooting facilities (in other words, instead of flying a crew out of New York or Chicago to shoot in your area, why not use you instead and save some money), then you can take advantage of the big metropolitan market fees. But you must be able to offer something that is comparable to

New York or Chicago or Los Angeles, or is unique to you.

As either an illustrator or photographer, you must be near an airport. If you live in an area that does not have regular air service into the major metropolitan areas, it is going to be almost impossible to do business in these areas. Deadlines can be tight, and losing that extra day while the freight service forwards your sketch or artwork, by truck, from a major city airport to you in a small, outlying town just will not work.

In addition to air freight accessibility, you should purchase or have access to a FAX machine. A FAX machine transmits via the telephone anything that is printed on a page (your large sketch will be conveniently reduced to an 8 1/2 by 11 inch size to fit the copier). Material is transmitted instantly to a compatible receiver in another city. The art director does not have to wait overnight for his sketch. Unfortunately, you cannot transmit art finishes this way, and also the presentation is not nearly as dramatic as a carefully-drawn sketch, beautifully mounted and sent by air freight. But a FAX machine can save time when time is critical and should be used if one is available to you.

You should be working in an illustrative or photographic style that is unique and cannot readily be bought in New York or other major metropolitan areas. If you are doing what everyone else is doing in New York, why should the art director put up with the aggravation and unforeseen problems that may arise if he buys out-of-town talent, when he could buy the very same thing in New York?

On the other hand, if you are a good photorealistic painter and have the "head" for paperbacks, you can live on the banks of the Nile and still work in the paperback field, because your style is always in demand in New York and other areas where paperback art is bought.

If you are a photographer, again, offer the specialty that cannot be bought anywhere else. (Underwater photography is a perfect example. New York's polluted rivers do not easily lend themselves to underwater exoticism).

To be candid, if you live outside one of the major metropolitan areas, you are going to lose some work, regardless of how good you are and the kind of specialty you have. First, most of the weekly magazines are going to eliminate you, because of their tight deadlines (particularly when it comes to covers), and because of the art director's need to work personally with the illustrator in orchestrating cover art that deals with fast-breaking news events.

Secondly, a great deal of advertising work is automatically lost to you, particularly if the deadline is under three days from start to finish (Remember: air freight automatically loses you two days — one day coming and one day going). And corrections are often a lost cause with out-of-town talent.

Third, there are art directors who refuse, purely on psychological grounds, to deal with any illustrator or photographer out-of-town. These art directors feel that the pressure is just not worth the hassle unless they cannot buy the talent locally.

On the plus side, however, many major magazines do not object to using out-of-town talent. Magazine deadlines, particularly for fiction pieces, are usually much more flexible than advertising or weekly magazine deadlines, and many out-of-town illustrators tap these editorial markets for additional income and national prestige.

WORKING WITHOUT AN AGENT

Suppose that you cannot obtain an agent in any of the major metropolitan markets (and they are in very short supply in all areas, including New York), how do you get ready for the New York, Chicago, Atlanta, or Los Angeles market business on your own?

- First of all, get set up for business before you get into business. Make arrangements with a local messenger service that will keep one or two of your portfolios available so they can deliver them when you give the word. Not an ideal arrangement because the portfolio cannot be "tailored" to each sales call, but better than no portfolio at all. No original paintings should be kept in these portfolios — only transparencies and tear sheets. A messenger service can put your portfolio within minutes of a possible job.

- Maintain a local answering service in New York or elsewhere that can take messages for you. When you send out your promotional mailings to all the agencies, magazines, and other prospects, list this local New York telephone number. All of a sudden, you are a New York, locally-based illustrator or photographer, at least as far as that initial art director contact is concerned. Follow-up with your own personal phone call after you have received your messages from your answering service. Remember: your messenger service can quickly dispatch your portfolio to that "hot" prospect.

PRACTICAL TIPS FOR SERVICING THE MARKET

Use some of these practical tips that will save you time and overcome potential problems:

- Getting the finished artwork to the client: There are many experienced and dependable services which can guarantee delivery of your artwork to big city clients. These range from the US Post Office Express Mail Service, which offers next day delivery of packages either from post office to post office, or post office to addressee; to air freight services such as Federal Express, which will pick up at your door and deliver the next morning, the next afternoon, or within two days to your client; to domestic airlines which offer small package express service (packages must be brought to and picked up at the airport); to special emergency delivery services that will deliver your artwork on the very same day you send it (expensive, but worth it if the client needs your artwork now).

  Also, before you use any outside freight services, always check with your client about their own "in-house" delivery systems. Large publishers, major networks, international agencies, etc., often have their own internal dispatching services, and you may find that if you can get your artwork to a branch or subsidiary office of a client, they will take care of expediting it for you.

- When you airfreight a sketch, always keep a copy for yourself, so you don't waste a day sending the sketch back and forth to the art director. If you and the art director both have a copy of the same sketch, any changes or additions and, most important, approval can be instantly given over the phone.

- Pack art in heavy cardboard or styrofoam and pack it very, very well. Accidents can and do happen, and even though air freight is normally insured, insurance money doesn't do the art director any good when your damaged artworks makes him late for his magazine closing.

- Shoot an 8-by-10 transparency or, at the very least, a 35mm slide of your finished job before you ship it to the art director (a good practice to follow regardless of whether you are out-of-town or not). Using transparencies is critical, of course, when dealing with overseas clients, since original art carries a very high tariff. Changes can be made by you on the original painting and a new transparency shot and sent overseas. But it is always a good idea to keep a transparency record for yourself of all jobs you do. Once that piece of art is gone to New York, it may be lost forever.

- Ask the art director if you can charge for air freight. Sometimes the client will assume all freight expenses; other times, the client will pay only when a piece of art is reshipped to you for corrections. Telephone calls to the art director are at your expense. Who pays for what, by the way, should always be resolved before the job is started so there is no misunderstanding.

- Always keep time on your mind when doing a job for an out-of-town client. Since there is usually a twenty-four-hour "loss" involved when using air freight, you should finish your painting at least one day earlier and sooner if possible, just in case corrections are needed. Remember: as an out-of-town artist working in the New York or other metropolitan markets, you are always on the line. The time demands on you are much greater than the in-town illustrator. Make sure you keep giving that New York art director reasons for having the good sense to choose you over local illustrators.

- Keep good relationships with the key personnel at the air freight service and your local post office express mail window. They can help you locate that hard-to-find or overdue package and avoid all kinds of art director problems.

- And finally, keep your cool. There will be days when everything goes wrong, but, because you are hundreds or even thousands of miles away, there is not much you can do about it. Don't panic. Be honest with the art director. Try to get him to help (for example, if there is a delivery problem, the art director might be able to expedite things at his end). Just stay in control at all times.

On the reverse side, there will be days when absolutely everything goes right, and you will wonder why you didn't exploit these big metropolitan markets years ago. It all evens out in the end.

A final word of advice: Never lie to the art director about where you are located and whether you are representing yourself or have an agent. Yes, you might lose that job because you are located outside New York, but it is much more professional to turn your out-of-town location into a positive selling point than it is to deceive the art director into thinking you are locally based. It is one thing to set up for business in a large metropolitan area. It is quite another thing to hide your out-of-town location just for the sake of a job.

If an art director wants to use you and you tell him that you are located out-of-town and why that is no great problem, chances are he will still use you. But you can imagine the art director's chagrin and anger when he expects you at a nine o'clock meeting in the client's office and then finds out you are hundreds of miles away. That kind of deception just doesn't work, and, as a professional illustrator or photographer, you should never do it.

NOW A WORD ABOUT EXPENSE

It is expensive for an illustrator or photographer to sell effectively in the New York or other major markets. Long distance telephone calls have a way of eating up a budget. Air freight costs are rising every year. Messenger and answering service costs are constantly going up. If you are forced to make one or more trips a year into New York, then you can add hotels, air fare, and entertainment costs to your out-of-town selling expenses.

As an illustrator or photographer, you must take a realistic look at how much business you are going to get out of a place like New York, compared to what it is costing you to get that business. For example, if you find that you are doing exactly the same kind of work in New York as you are doing in Milwaukee, where you live, yet the expenses of producing and servicing that New York work is costing a disproportionate amount, it may be the time to cease and desist as far as the New York market is concerned.

On the other hand, if you are doing beautiful illustrations for national magazines headquartered in New York or Chicago, chances are that the money received for these jobs, as well as the satisfaction and recognition you receive, is well worth the expense.

Obviously, if getting work from a large metropolitan market is materially adding to your income while, at the same time, enhancing your artistic reputation, it is definitely worthwhile to continue working in these large markets.

As previously mentioned, it will also cost you money to get an agent in these large metropolitan markets. That extra 5 or 10 percent commission (30 to 35 percent as compared to 25 percent) can be significant to the illustrator or photographer. And yet it is becoming increasingly necessary to charge this additional commission percentage to service out-of-town talent. There is more long-distance telephoning between an agent and the talent he represents. The agent must cover the cost of sending artwork by air freight back to the artist if the client will not absorb these costs, and that comes right off the top. The agent may spend more time servicing — not selling — accounts for an out-of-town illustrator or photographer because the agent must become more personally involved in the everyday details of the job itself — things that an in-town talent might very well handle himself. It costs more to launch and maintain the career of an out-of-town talent than it does for a New York located artist or photographer and so most agents will charge more for this. From your point of view, that 30 to 35 percent commission you pay an agent comes right off the top of every job you do and, added on to the already heavy freight, telephone, and other expenses, further reduces your profit.

After all is said and done, if you really want to expand your talents and break into the major metropolitan markets, do it. Nothing is insurmountable. It may cost you money to do it, but if you have something to sell and are willing to work hard and take some chances, the rewards for the out-of-town talent, both financially and artistically, can be gratifying.

How Long Does it Take To Succeed?

8

We all know that the free-lance business has a Las Vegas quality to it. Stay in it long enough and you will experience the thrill of getting a big job, a big break, for simply being in the right place at the right time. We've all gone through a lean period feeling just about ready to switch into another field of work only to have the phone ring with an assignment that is second only to winning the lottery. And we have all witnessed or been involved with the recently graduated art student who is truly the overnight sensation. But these are the exceptions in this business and not the day-to-day reality.

Fifteen or twenty years ago it was much easier to start making a living in the business within a year or two. There were fewer free-lancers, more work, and better prices. There were large studio situations and many entry level jobs at ad agencies that enabled beginning free-lancers to supplement their incomes while establishing their careers.

And there were campaigns (remember those?), one and two-year assignments from agencies, whose accounts were more permanent. The very first job we sold as beginning representatives was a year's campaign of photography trade ads to be shot every week. Because fees were so good, we didn't itemize expenses. No one took bids or estimates. We sealed the deal with a handshake and only after we were well into the campaign did we bother to get purchase orders. The commissions on that one campaign were easily enough to pay our bills for the year. The rest of the year was gravy.

Now, because of the overcrowded marketplace, the oversupply of free-lancers, the mergers and acquisitions, account switches, the changes in pricing and the new usage situations, it takes a minimum of two years to even learn what the business is buying and what they're paying for it.

During the first two years, the jobs are usually spotty, not well paying, and offer little if any repeat business. And even the most gifted free-lancers need time to develop the hands-on experience of learning their capacity for producing, as well as those tricks and shortcuts that improve their productivity while not diminishing quality. They need to experiment, as well as grow in their knowledge of their art.

New free-lancers often go with new representatives, and both parties are in effect getting on-the-job training. This can prolong the process of getting established.

Cash flow is another consideration. If a free-lancer gets one job during the first three months in the field, it may take a month or more to complete the assignment and bill it, and anywhere from one to three months more to get paid. It can take years to generate any kind of even cash flow.

In today's market, it takes a minimum of three years for most free-lancers to begin earning a livable wage. Five years to establish a business is not unreasonable, and to get into a healthy financial bracket, which includes a high income, good repeat business, and a following of some kind, can easily take ten years in today's economy. This may sound grim, but it is reality and the person who prepares for reality is better able to survive and beat the odds.

There is a positive side to this, however. Many poorly trained and minimally talented people have flooded the field, as opposed to many years ago. And with all of the layoffs in the business, many unemployed people free-lance because they cannot find a regular job, further adding to the oversupply. Therefore, this oversupply of underqualified free-lancers makes the truly talented individual not only stand out, but eventually be sought out. Good talent is in demand as never before and will be more in demand in the future.

How does the beginning free-lancer survive those early years? Somehow, one has to have some kind of financial reserves. We often say to beginning free-lancers, only half-jokingly, live with your parents, marry well, get a wealthy girlfriend, boyfriend, patron, or get a part-time job to see you through those lean years.

If you are still in those early, struggling years, you actually may not be failing, but may be on schedule in your quest to establish yourself as a free-lance entrepreneur. It may take longer than you anticipated and hoped.

If you have talent, can produce efficiently, find the means to support yourself initially, and persist in your endeavors — you'll succeed.

Addendum

PROFESSIONAL ORGANIZATIONS AND ASSOCIATIONS

Advertising Photographers of America (APA)
27 West 20th Street
New York, NY 10011

Photographers specializing in all aspects of the advertising business.

American Institute of Graphic Arts (AIGA)
1059 Third Avenue
New York, NY 10021

Leading organization for display, publication, and preservation of general graphic and design works in printed media.

American Society of Magazine Photographers (ASMP)
419 Park Avenue South
New York, NY 10016

Photographers working in communication media, including advertising, industrial, journalism, and related fields. Has chapters in Atlanta, Boston, Chicago, Houston, Los Angeles, New York, Philadelphia, San Francisco, and Seattle.

Art Directors Club (of New York)
250 Park Avenue South
New York, NY 10003

Sponsor of major national advertising and Corporate art directing award show; exhibits and publishes work of excellence in that field. Art Directors Clubs in Boston, Connecticut, New Jersey, Philadelphia, and many other areas perform similar functions on a local level.

Artists Equity Association
P.O. Box 28068
Central Station
Washington, DC 20038

Deals with issues generally affecting rights of artists, with primary emphasis on the fine arts. There are 10 regional branches of AEA located throughout the United States.

Artists Equity Association of New York
32 Union Square East Rm #1103
New York, NY 10003

Concerned with issues affecting artists' (primarily fine artists') rights.

Cartoonist Association
54 East 3rd Street
New York, NY 10012

Concerned with the professional standards of free-lance cartoonists.

The Graphic Artists Guild (GAG)
11 West 20th Street
New York, New York 10011

The leading national organization for the promotion and protection of graphic designers and illustrators in all areas, with legislation, publications, information, and group insurance programs. Chapters are active in Atlanta, Boston, Dallas, Greensboro (NC), Honolulu, Long Island, Los Angeles, Miami, Nashville, New York, Orange County (CA), St. Louis, Salt Lake City, San Francisco, and Seattle.

Publications include the landmark volume Pricing and Ethical Guidelines.

In addition, the Guild sponsors a wide array of seminars and works that are of vital importance to graphic artists. Contact the national headquarters for details.

International Center of Photography (ICP)
1130 5th Avenue
New York, NY 10028

Primarily a leading cultural organization that also offers a number of seminars and courses that may be of interest to professionals.

The Joint Ethics Committee (JEC)
P.O. Box 179
Grand Central Station
New York, NY 10017

Mediates or arbitrates disputes between graphic artists and clients. Has done so successfully for some 35 years. Sponsored jointly by the Art Directors Club of New York, the American Society of Magazine Photographers, the Graphic Artists Guild, the Society of Illustrators, and the Society of Photographers and Artists Representatives.

Professional Photographers of America (PPA)
1090 Executive Way
Des Plaines, IL 60018

Portrait, wedding, commercial, and industrial photographers. PPA has chapters and affiliates throughout the country in each of these disciplines. Contact the National Office for details.

The Society of Illustrators
128 East 63rd Street
New York, NY 10022

Leading cultural force in the preservation of works of past illustrators and in the exhibition, publication, and preservation of works of living illustrators; active social and educational programs for illustrators, other members of the public interested in the art form, and students of art and illustration; sponsors the leading show of current work in the field and the basic visual reference book for the industry, both titled Illustrators Annual. *Societies of Illustrators in other cities such as Los Angeles are important in their area but are not directly affiliated.*

Society of Publication Designers
60 East 42nd Street Suite 1416
New York, NY 10165

Sponsors education meetings and the leading national annual exhibition and publication in the field of publication design.

Society of Artists and Photographers Representatives (SPAR)
1123 Broadway, Suite 914
New York, NY 10012

Primarily New York-based representatives of artists, photographers, and some designers; sponsors educational programs for members and representatives just entering field; and supplies members with a current list of advertising art directors in New York City.

Type Directors Club
60 East 42nd Street Suite 1416
New York, NY 10165

Concerned with professional standards and artistic achievements in the field of type design and utilization; sponsors the major national show and new annual publication on these subjects.

Visual Artists and Galleries Association (VAGA)
One Rockefeller Plaza, 26th Floor
New York, NY 10020

Concerned with marketing and preserving rights for reproduction of both fine and commercial art works.

Volunteer Lawyers for the Arts (VLA)
1285 Avenue of the Americas
New York, NY 10019

Provides free legal services to individuals and organizations satisfying its income requirements; can direct you to similar services in a number of other cites including Chicago, San Francisco, and Houston.

DIRECTORIES

ASMP Membership Directory
American Society of Magazine Photographers
419 Park Avenue South
New York, NY 10016
Published in 1985, this directory includes more than 2,800 listings of photographers world-wide composing the ASMP general and associate membership. Listings are categorized by geographic area and include specialties.

Adweek Directory of Advertising
Adweek
49 East 21st Street
New York, NY 10010
The Directory of Advertising is a reference guide to clients, agencies, and media in 5 regional volumes. Listings include addresses, phone numbers, and key contacts. Each volume contains over 300 pages and is published annually each fall.

The Adweek Portfolios
Adweek
49 East 21st St.
New York, NY 10010
Design, Commercial Production, and a Creative Services Index. The Portfolios are presented both nationally and internationally. The U.S. volume also appears in the hard-bound international edition.

The American Register of Printing & Graphic Arts Services
1485 Bayshore Blvd.
San Francisco, CA 94124
The American Register is a national sourcebook for printing and graphic arts services. Published annually, it is available by mail order.

American Showcase
724 Fifth Avenue
New York, NY 10019
An extensive color survey of current graphic designers, commercial photographers, and illustrators. The publication functions as a promotional medium to reach potential national and international clients. This annual compendium is open to qualified artists and suppliers and is available in local book and art supply stores.

Art Directors Annual
Art Directors Club
250 Park Avenue South
New York, NY 10003
A directory of outstanding print and television advertising, reflecting the creativity of some of the top art directors in the business.

Chicago Talent Sourcebook
Alexander Communications
212 West Superior #400
Chicago, IL 60610
This is a comprehensive guide and portfolio of illustration, design, and photography from the Chicago area.

Corporate Showcase
724 Fifth Avenue
New York, NY 10019
Corporate Showcase *is a color survey of corporate photography and advertising illustration on a national level and is available in local book and art supply stores.*

The Creative Black Book
115 Fifth Avenue
New York, NY 10003
Directory of top photographers and illustrators servicing all markets, both nationally and internationally.

The Madison Avenue Handbook
Peter Glenn Publications
17 East 48th Street
New York, NY 10017
This four-color directory has 22 sections and over 25,000 listings, including ad agencies and personnel, TV and music producers, photographers, illustrators, and animation and special effects suppliers.

RSVP The Directory of Creative Talent
P.O. Box 314
Brooklyn, NY 11205
This national collection of promotional pieces from illustrators, designers, and photographers is published annually and distributed internationally.

The Red Books
National Register Publishing Company
866 Third Avenue
New York, NY 10022
The Red Books *provide essential marketing facts on over 17,000 corporations and 4,400 advertising agencies.*

SRDS
Standard Rate and Data Service
866 Third Avenue
New York, NY 10022
SRDS books are the most complete media source available. Contents include markets, contacts, rates, coverage, circulation, closing, and publishing requirements. Twelve separate volumes may be purchased on a subscription basis or as single copies. The issues include business publications, newspapers, magazines, spot television and radio, direct mail lists, community publications, plus Canadian and international rates and data.

Society of Illustrators Annual Show Directory
128 East 63rd Street
New York, NY 10022
This book contains the award-winning entries of the Society of Illustrator's annual show.

MAGAZINES

ADVERTISING AGE

740 Rush Street
Chicago, IL 60611

AD WEEK

49 East 21st Street
New York, NY 10010

AMERICAN ARTIST

One Astor Plaza
New York, NY 10036

AMERICAN PHOTOGRAPHER

1515 Broadway
New York, NY 10036

ART DIRECTION MAGAZINE

10 East 39th Street
New York, NY 10016

COMMUNICATION ARTS

P.O. Box 10300
Palo Alto, CA 94303

CREATIVITY

220 East 42nd Street
New York, NY 10017

HOW

1507 Dana Avenue
Cincinnati, OH 45207

GRAPHIC DESIGN: USA

120 East 56th Street
New York, NY 10022

MODERN PHOTOGRAPHY

825 Seventh Avenue
New York, NY 10019

PETERSEN'S PHOTOGRAPHIC

8490 Sunset Boulvard
Los Angeles, CA 90291

PHOTO DISTRICT NEWS

49 East 21st Street
New York, NY 10010

POPULAR PHOTOGRAPHY

One Park Avenue
New York, NY 10016

PRINT MAGAZINE

104 5th Avenue
New York, NY 10011

U&lc

2 Hammarskjold P!aza
New York, NY 10017

FORMS FOR FREE-LANCERS

Following are examples of useful forms that can help free-lancers better control art and photography assignments.

Free-lancers wishing to get a broader range of forms can write to SPAR at 1123 Broadway, Room 914, New York, NY 10010, and request the "Do-It-Yourself Rep Kit" for either photographers or artists.

The model release form and the confirmation of assignment form for illustrators are taken from *Business and Legal forms for Illustrators* by Tad Crawford (Allworth Press, distributed by North Light Books).

Release Form for Models

In consideration of ____________________ Dollars ($__________), receipt of which is acknowledged, I, ____________________, do hereby give ____________________, his or her assigns, licensees, and legal representatives the irrevocable right to use my name (or any fictional name), picture, portrait, or photograph in all forms and media and in all manners, including composite or distorted representations, for advertising, trade, or any other lawful purposes, and I waive any right to inspect or approve the finished version(s), including written copy that may be created in connection therewith. I am of full age.* I have read this release and am fully familiar with its contents.

Witness____________________ Model____________________

Address____________________ Address____________________

Date __________, 19 ___

Consent (if applicable)

I am the parent or guardian of the minor named above and have the legal authority to execute the above release. I approve the foregoing and waive any rights in the premises.

Witness____________________ Parent or Guardian____________________

Address____________________ Address____________________

Date __________, 19 ___

* Delete this sentence if the subject is a minor. The parent or guardian must then sign the consent.

Confirmation of Assignment

AGREEMENT as of the _____ day of ___________, 19 _____, between ______________________________,
(hereinafter referred to as the "Client"), located at ______________________________,
and ______________________________ (hereinafter referred to as the "Illustrator"),
located at ______________________________, with
respect to the creation of certain illustrations (hereinafter referred to as the "Work").

WHEREAS, Illustrator is a professional illustrator of good standing;

WHEREAS, Client wishes the Illustrator to create certain Work described more fully herein; and

WHEREAS, Illustrator wishes to create such Work;

NOW, THEREFORE, in consideration of the foregoing premises and the mutual covenants hereinafter set forth and other valuable considerations, the parties hereto agree as follows:

1. **Description.** The Illustrator agrees to create the Work in accordance with the following specifications:

   Subject matter ______________________________

   Number of illustrations in color ______________________________

   Number of illustrations in black and white ______________________________

   Size of illustrations ______________________________

   Medium for illustrations ______________________________

   Other specifications ______________________________

   Client purchase order number ______________________________ Job number ______________

2. **Due Date.** The Illustrator agrees to deliver sketches within _____ days after the later of the signing of this Agreement or, if the Client is to provide reference, layouts, or specifications, after the Client has provided same to the Illustrator. Finished art shall be delivered _____ days after the approval of sketches by the Client.

3. **Grant of Rights.** Upon receipt of full payment, the Illustrator grants to the Client the following rights in the finished art:

   For use as ______________________________

   For the product or publication named ______________________________

   In the following territory ______________________________

   For the following time period ______________________________

   Other limitations ______________________________

   With respect to the usage shown above, the Client shall have ❑ exclusive ❑ nonexclusive rights.

   If the finished art is for use as a contribution to a magazine, the grant of rights shall be for first North American serial rights only unless specified to the contrary above.

4. **Reservation of Rights**. All rights not expressly granted hereunder are reserved to the Illustrator, including but not limited to all rights in sketches, comps, or other preliminary materials.

5. **Fee.** Client agrees to pay the following purchase price: $_______ for the usage rights granted. Client agrees to pay sales tax, if required.

6. **Additional Usage.** If Client wishes to make any additional uses of the Work, Client agrees to seek permission from the Illustrator and make such payments as are agreed to between the parties at that time.

7. **Expenses.** Client agrees to reimburse the Illustrator for the following expenses: ❑ Messengers ❑ Models ❑ Props ❑ Travel ❑ Telephone ❑ Other ______________________________

   At the time of signing this Agreement, Client shall pay Illustrator $_______ as a nonrefundable advance against expenses. If the advance exceeds expenses incurred, the credit balance shall be used to reduce the fee payable or, if the fee has been fully paid, shall be reimbursed to Client.

8. **Payment.** Client agrees to pay the Illustrator within thirty days of the date of Illustrator's billing, which shall be dated as of the date of delivery of the finished art. In the event that work is postponed at the request of the Client, the Illustrator shall have the right to bill pro rata for work completed through the date of that request, while reserving all other rights under this Agreement. Overdue payments shall be subject to interest charges of _____ percent monthly.
9. **Advances.** At the time of signing this Agreement, Client shall pay Illustrator ____ percent of the fee as an advance against the total fee. Upon approval of sketches Client shall pay Illustrator ____ percent of the fee as an advance against the total fee.
10. **Revisions.** The Illustrator shall be given the first opportunity to make any revisions requested by the Client. If the revisions are not due to any fault on the part of the Illustrator, an additional fee shall be charged. If the Illustrator objects to any revisions to be made by the Client, the Illustrator shall have the right to have his or her name removed from the published Work.
11. **Copyright Notice.** Copyright notice in the Illustrator's name ❑ shall ❑ shall not be published with the Work.
12. **Authorship Credit.** Authorship credit in the name of the Illustrator ❑ shall ❑ shall not accompany the Work when it is reproduced. If the finished art is used as a contribution to a magazine or for a book, authorship credit shall be given unless specified to the contrary in the preceding sentence.
13. **Cancellation.** In the event of cancellation by the Client, the following cancellation payment shall be paid by the Client: **(A)** Cancellation prior to the finished art being turned in: ____% of fee; **(B)** Cancellation due to finished art being unsatisfactory: ____% of fee; and **(C)** Cancellation for any other reason after the finished art is turned in: ____% of fee. In the event of cancellation, the Client shall also pay any expenses incurred by the Illustrator and the Illustrator shall own all rights in the Work. The billing upon cancellation shall be payable within thirty days of the Client's notification to stop work or the delivery of the finished art, whichever occurs sooner.
14. **Ownership and Return of Artwork.** The ownership of original artwork, including sketches and any other materials created in the process of making the finished art, shall remain with the Illustrator. All such artwork shall be returned to the Illustrator by bonded messenger, air freight, or registered mail within thirty days of the Client's completing its use of the artwork. The parties agree that the value of the original, finished art is $______.
15. **Permissions and Releases.** The Client agrees to indemnify and hold harmless the Illustrator against any and all claims, costs, and expenses, including attorney's fees, due to materials included in the Work at the request of the Client for which no copyright permission or privacy release was requested or uses which exceed the uses allowed pursuant to a permission or release.
16. **Arbitration.** All disputes arising under this Agreement shall be submitted to binding arbitration before ____________________ in the following location ________________________ and settled in accordance with the rules of the American Arbitration Association. Judgment upon the arbitration award may be entered in any court having jurisdiction thereof. Disputes in which the amount at issue is less than $___________ shall not be subject to this arbitration provision.
17. **Miscellany.** This Agreement shall be binding upon the parties hereto, their heirs, successors, assigns, and personal representatives. This Agreement constitutes the entire understanding between the parties. Its terms can be modified only by an instrument in writing signed by both parties, except that the Client may authorize expenses or revisions orally. A waiver of a breach of any of the provisions of this Agreement shall not be construed as a continuing waiver of other breaches of the same or other provisions hereof. This Agreement shall be governed by the laws of the State of __________________.

IN WITNESS WHEREOF, the parties hereto have signed this Agreement as of the date first set forth above.

Illustrator ______________________________ Client ______________________________
Company Name

By ______________________________
Authorized Signatory, Title

Job Title/Product________________ Date________ JOB#________ ☐ ESTIMATE
Client________________ ☐ INVOICE

STUDIO EXPENSES

Coordinator .... ______days ________
Assistant(s) .... ______days ________
Other________________ ________
Special Equipment .... ________
Special Facilities .... ________
Studio Props .... ________
Polaroid .... ________
Color Film and Processing ...... ________
B/W Film/Processing/Contacts .. ________
Miscellaneous Material(s) .... ________
Catering .... ________
Insurance .... ________
Air Freight/Truckin .... ________
Messengers/Express Delivery .... ________
Postage/Telephone/etc .... ________
Estimated Model Time .... ________
Studio-paid Models (Invoice) .... ________
Casting .... ________
____Adults ____Children
____Animals ____Trainers
Polaroids .... ________
Use of Casting Files .... ________
Stylist .... ______days ________
Expenses .... ________
Props .... ________
Wardrobe .... ________
Hair/Make-up .... ______days ________
Home Economist ...... ______days ________
Food-stuff .... ________
Model Maker .... ________
Set Designer .... ________
Expenses .... ________
Set Rental(s) .... ________
Set Construction .... ________
Other________________ ________

TOTAL STUDIO EXPENSES ...... ________

QUOTED FEES (CDR)________

Creative Fee .... ______days ________
Experimental Fee ...... ______days ________
Corp-Indus ______per day______days ________
Photomatic ______per day______days ________
Prep/Research .... ______days ________
Strike/Post Production .. ______days ________
Travel .... ______days ________
Weather .... ______days ________
Postponement/Delay ... ______days ________
Other________________ ________
Production Charges ______% ..... ________

TOTAL PHOTOGRAPHER FEE(S) . ________

LOCATION EXPENSES

Coordinator .... ______days ________
Assistant(s) .... ______days ________
Other________________ ________
Special Equipment .... ________
Special Facilities .... ________
Studio Props .... ________
Polaroid .... ________
Color Film and Processing ...... ________
B/W Film/Processing/Contacts .. ________
Miscellaneous Material(s) ...... ________
Catering .... ________
Insurance .... ________
Air Freight/Trucking .... ________
Messengers/Express Delivery .... ________
Postage/Telephone/etc .... ________
Estimated Model Time .... ________
Studio-paid Models (Invoice) .... ________
Casting .... ________
____Adults ____Children
____Animals ____Trainers
Polaroids .... ________
Use of Casting Files .... ________
Stylist .... ______days ________
Expenses .... ________
Props .... ________
Wardrobe .... ________
Hair/Make-up .... ______days ________
Home Economist ..... ______days ________
Food-stuff .... ________
Location Scout .... ______days ________
Expenses .... ________
Other________________ ________
Permits & Permissions .... ________
Use of Location Files .... ________
Location Rental ...... ______days ________
Location Van .... ______days ________
Car/Truck Rentals .... ________
Helicopters/Pack Mules etc .... ________
Cherry Picker/Scaffolding/etc ...... ________
Air Fare/Other Fares .... ________
Overweight Baggage .... ________
Airport Transfers/Taxis .... ________
Per Diem ______per day ______days . ________
Lodging______ nights .... ________
Meals .... ________
Gratuities .... ________
Other Expenses________________ ________

TOTAL LOCATION EXPENSES ... ________

TOTAL FEES AND EXPENSES ________

Index

A

Additional usage fee, 82, 83
Advances, 79, 92, 93
Advertising market, 11-14. *See also* Art directors
  art buyer and, 14
  art director and, 14
  collateral promotion and, 12
  color and, 33
  corporate, 18
  coupon, 20
  department store, 22-23, 36
  directories and, 60-61
  fashion, 23
  industrial, 12
  local, 12
  location of, 13-14
  magazines and, 11-12
  mergers and, 16
  movies and, 20-21
  national consumer, 11-12
  newspaper, 12, 20
  out-of-town artists and photographers and, 106
  pharmaceutical, 12-13
  promotion and direct response, 13
  stock photography and, 24-25
  television, 21, 24
Agents. *See* Artist agents
American Showcase, 59
American Society of Magazine Photographers (ASMP), 77
American Society of Magazine Photographers (ASMP) Business Practices in Photography, 80
Animatics, 29
Annual reports, 18, 19,
  portfolio and, 37
  pricing and, 84
  answering service, 91
  out-of-town artists and photographers and, 107, 109
Art buyer, 14
Art directors, 14
  artist agents and, 95-96
  letters to, 69
  magazines and, 16
  paperbacks and, 15
  personal calls to, 65, 67-69
  retail catalogs and, 23
  speaking to groups of, 69
Art Directors' Club, 63
Artist agents, 95-101
  activities of, 96
  art directors and, 95-96
  billing and, 98
  as brokers, 98
  compensating, 97-98
  contract with, 100-1
  expenses and, 98-99
  interviewing, 96, 101
  key questions to ask, 101
  need for, 99-100
  new, 112
  out-of-town artists and photographers and, 97, 104-5, 109-10
  publishing and, 15
  termination agreement with, 100-1
  where and how to find, 95-96
Art packages, 15
Art studios, 19
Associations and organizations, professional, 113-14
Audio/visual firms, 19-20

B

Beauty photography, 33, 55
  portfolio and, 36-37
Billing and collecting, 92-94
  artist agents and, 98
  copyrights and reproduction rights and, 94
Black and white illustration or photography, 20
  beauty photography, 37
  in portfolio, 33
  small promotional pieces, 64, 69
Black Book, 59
Books. *See also* Publishing market.
  writing and illustrating your own, 15
Boy/girl sample, 31
  illustration, 39
  photography, 54
Broadway theater, 21
Brokers, artist agents as, 98
Business matters
  billing and collecting, 92-94, 98
  cash flow, 112
  checklist for, 94
  corporations and, 89-90, 94
  forms, 118-22
  office help, 91-92
  overhead, 91, 94
  partnerships and sole proprietorships and, 90-91, 94
  record keeping, 91, 94
Buy-out, 87

C

Calendars, 25
  promotional, 65
Cash flow, 112
"C" corporations, 89-90, 94
Celebrity portrait, 36
Collateral promotion, 12, 13
Color, in portfolio, 33
Commission
  artist agents, 97-98
  stock photography and, 24-25
Computer graphics, 24
Conference fee, 77
Confirmation of assignment form, 119-20
Contracts
  with artist agents, 100-1
  poster and calendar art and, 25
  stock photography and, 24-25
Copyrights and reproduction rights, 86-88
  billing and collecting and, 94
  buy-out and, 87
  poster and calendar art and, 25
  pricing and, 78
Corporate market, 17-19, 53
  directory for, 63
  portfolio and, 37
  pricing and, 84
Coupon advertising, 20

D

Deadline
  out-of-town artists and photographers and, 105, 106, 108
  pricing and, 76
Department store advertising, 22-23, 36
Design studios, 19
Direct mail, 59
Directories, 115-16
  pages from, as promotional pieces, 66, 74
  promotion in, 59-60
Direct response agencies, 13

E

Editorial art, 32, 33
  illustration, 46
  photography, 52
Editorial directory, 61
Exhibiting your work, 69
Expenses, 77
  artist agents and, 98-99
  form for, 121
  out-of-town artists and photographers and, 109-10
  pricing and, 86

F

Fashion market
  advertising agencies and, 23
  department store advertising, 22-23, 36
  illustration and, 49
  magazines, 23
  models and, 35
  photography and, 35, 36, 55
  retail catalogs and, 23
FAX machines, 91, 106
Feature writer and syndicate directory, 61, 63
Finish fees, 82, 83
Florida, 14
Fold-out mailers, 63-64, 72
Form 1099, 92, 98
Forms, business, 118-22

G

Gebbie House Magazine Directory, 63
General trade publishing, 14-15
  pricing and, 81

H

Hairdressers, 37
House accounts, 98

I

Illustration. *See also specific topics*
  boy/girl sample, 39
  editorial sample, 46
  fashion sample, 49
  industrial sample, 43
  medical, 13
  movie sample, 42
  national consumer agencies and, 12
  paperback sample, 41
  pharmaceutical sample, 47
  photorealistic, 15-16, 20, 77
  portfolio, 39-50
  product sample, 44
  public relations firms and, 19
  publishing and, 15
  retail catalogs and, 23
  slice-of-life sample, 45
  specialized product, 32, 44
  sport sample, 48
  travel sample, 40
Industrial advertising agencies, 12
Industrial photography, 18
Industrial sample, 32, 43
In-store merchandising, 13

J

Joint Ethics Committee (JEC), 100

K

Kill fees, 84

L

Leave-behind promotional pieces, 30, 68
Legal Guide for the Visual Artist (Crawford), 87
Legal action, collection and, 93-94
Letters to art directors, 69
Lighting, fashion photography and, 36
Literary Market Place, 61
Local advertising agencies, 12
Location, photography and, 36
Low-balling, 75-76

M

Magazines, 16-17
  advertising in, 11-12
  corporate in-house, 17-18
  directory for, 61
  fashion, 23
  free promotion in, 65
  out-of-town artists and photographers and, 106-7
  photography and, 17
  pricing and, 80-81
  promotion and, 58-59
  special interest, 17
  trade, 58-59, 117
Mailing house, 62
Mailing lists
  Advertising Agency Redbook, 60-61
  corporate market and, 63
  Literary Market Place, 61
  mailing house and, 62
  questions and answers about, 62
  Standard Directory of Advertisers, 61
  Working Press of the Nation, 61, 63
Make-up artists, 37
Markets. *See also specific topics*
  advertising, 11-14
  age of audience and, 37
  art studios, 19
  audio/visual firms, 19-20
  computer graphics, 24
  corporate, 18
  design studios, 19
  fashion, 22-24
  movie, 20-21
  newspaper advertising, 20
  posters and calendars, 25
  public relations firms, 19
  publishing, 14-16
  record album, cassette, and CD, 18
  researching, 17, 25-26
  sales promotion agencies, 18-19
  stock photography, 24-25
  TV networks, 21, 21
  TV storyboards, 24
Medical illustration, 13
Mergers, 16
Messenger service, out-of-

town artists and photographers and, 107, 109
Model release form, 122
Models, 35-37, 105
Movie art, 20-21, 31-32
illustration, 42
pricing, 82-83
Music market, 18

N

National consumer agencies, 11-12
fashion advertising and, 23
Newspapers
advertising and, 12, 20
directory for, 61
Sunday supplements in, 17
New York, 13
out-of-town artists and photographers, 103-10
paperback market in, 15
New York Society of Illustrators Annual Show Directory, 59-60

O

Office help, 91-92
Operating costs, 75. *See also* Overhead
Organizations and associations, professional, 113-14
Out-of-town artists and photographers, 103-10
advertising agencies 106
answering service and, 107, 109
artist agents and, 97, 104-5, 109-10
deadlines and, 105, 106, 108
expenses and, 109-10
FAX machine and, 106
lying to art directors about location, 109
magazines and, 106-7
messenger service and, 107, 109
promotion and, 107
shipping and, 105-10
telephone and, 109
Overhead, 91, 94
Oversized mailers, 64
Ownership. *See* Copyrights and reproduction rights

P

Paperback art, 15-16
pricing and, 81-82
sample, 31
illustration, 41
Partnerships, 90-91, 94
People photography
advertising and, 12
in annual reports, 18
celebrity portrait and, 36
models and, 35
pharmaceutical advertising and, 13
portfolio and, 35-36
retail catalogs and, 23
slice-of-life and, 35-36
Personal calls, 65, 67-69
Pharmaceutical art, 12-13
color in, 33
illustration sample, 47
Photographer agents. *See* Artist agents
Photography. *See also specific topics*
annual report, 18, 19, 53
beauty, 33, 36-37, 55
boy/girl, 54
editorial, 17, 52
fashion, 35, 36, 55
industrial, 18
magazines and, 17
movie art and, 21
national consumer agencies and, 12
paperbacks and, 16
people, 12, 13, 18, 12, 35-36
portfolio and, 34-38
product, 32, 51
publishing and, 15
reshoots, 85
retail catalogs and, 23
sales promotion agencies and, 19
slice-of-life, 35-36, 54
special effects, 12
still life, 12, 13, 23, 34-35, 51
stock, 24-25
stopper, 51
Photomatics, 29
Photorealism
expenses and, 77
movie art and, 20
paperback market and, 15-16
Photo stylist, 36
Portfolio, 27-56, 91
advertising vs. editorial pieces in, 33
animatics and, 29
black and white vs. color in, 33
dropping off, 67
duplicate, 29, 107
editing, 28
fashion photography, 35, 36
general guidelines for, 28-30
illustration, 39-50
number of samples in, 30
photography, 34-38
photomatics and, 29
physical presentation of, 28-29
promotional mailers and, 66
stoppers in, 34, 50, 51
structure of, 27-28
subject matter in, 30-34
tailoring to specific clients, 33-34
tear sheets in, 29
transparencies in, 29
Portfolio case, 29-30
Portrait photography, 31-32
magazines and, 17
Postcards, promotional, 73
Posters, 25, 64
Pricing, 75-88
advances and, 79, 92, 93
annual reports and, 84
billing and collecting and, 92-94
changes and, 84-85
client's budget and, 78-79
for color vs. black and white, 76
complexity of project and, 76-77
conference fee, 77
copyrights and reproduction rights and, 78, 86-88
deadline and, 76
expenses and, 77, 86
fair, 75
general trade books and, 81
guides to, 79-80
kill fees, 84
kind of project and, 76
low-balling and, 75-76
magazines and, 80-81

minimum, 75
mistakes in, 80, 86
movie art and, 82-83
on-the-spot, 86
operating costs and, 75
paperbacks and, 81-82
photography reshoots and, 85
purchase orders and, 85
single assignment vs. campaign and, 76
ten key questions about, 76-79
usage and, 78, 82, 83
Pricing and Ethical Guidelines, 80
Product art, 32
illustration, 44
photography, 51
Professional organizations and associations, 113-14
Promotion, 57-74. *See also* Artist agents; Promotional mailers
calendars and, 65
directories and, 59-60
free, 65
in magazines, 58-59, 65
out-of-town artists and photographers, 107
personal calls and, 65, 67-69
shows and exhibits and, 69
speaking engagements, 69
value of, 57-58
Promotion agencies, 13
Promotional mailers (promotional pieces), 63-65
black and white, small, 64
design and production tips for, 66
direct mail and, 59
directory pages and, 66, 74
examples of, 69-74
fold-out, 63-64, 71, 72
leave-behind, 30, 68
mailing lists and, 60-63
oversized, 64
portfolio and, 66
postcards, 73
posters, 64
specialized or selective, 62
tear sheets, 65
Public relations firms, 19
Publishing, 14-16. *See also* Magazines; *and specific topics*
general trade, 14-15
mergers and, 16
paperback, 15-16
special interest, 16
writing and illustrating your own book, 15
Purchase orders, 85

R

Radio and television directory, 61
Record album, cassette, and CD market, 18
Record keeping, 91, 94
Release form for models, 122
Repeat business, 12, 111, 112
corporate market and, 18
Representatives. *See* Artist agents
Reproduction rights. *See* Copyrights and reproduction rights
Retail catalogs, 23, 34
Royalties, poster and calendar art and, 25

S

Saachi & Saachi, 11
Sales promotion agencies, 18-19
Sales tax, 96, 98
"S" corporations, 89-90, 94
Shows and exhibits, promotion and, 69
Slice-of-life pieces, 32-33, 35-36
illustration, 45
photography, 54
Society of Illustrators, 69
Society of Photographers and Artists Representatives (SPAR), 95, 100, 105
Soft sculpture, 17, 99
Sole proprietorships, 90-91, 94
Speaking engagements, 69
Special effects photography, 12
Special interest books and magazines, 16, 17
Specialized product illustrator or photographer, 32
Sports illustration, 48
Standard Directory Of Advertisers, 61
Still-life photography, 51
advertising and, 12
pharmaceutical advertising and, 13
portfolio and, 34-35
retail catalogs and, 23, 34
Stock photography, 24-25
Stoppers, 34, 50, 51
Storyboards, television, 24
Success, achieving, 111-12
Survival, 112

T

Taxes, 90-92, 94
sales, 96, 98
Tearsheets, 29
as promotional pieces, 65
Telephone, 91
out-of-town artists and photographers and, 109
Television 21
advertising on, 12, 24
directory for, 61
fashion advertising and, storyboards, 24
Transparencies, 29
Travel photography, 31, 40

U

Usage, 78, 82, 83

W

Work for hire, 87
Working Press of the Nation, 61, 63

About the Authors

The husband and wife team of Elliott and Barbara Gordon are partners in their New York based firm of BARBARA GORDON ASSOCIATES, LTD., which represents some of the top commercial illustrators and photographers in the field today.

The couple has been the subject of major articles in *Communication Arts*, *New Woman Magazine*, and *Graphic Design: USA*.

Barbara Gordon has been on the Executive Board of the Society of Photographers and Artists Representatives (SPAR) for ten years and recently completed a term as President of the organization. She has also served as a member of the Steering Committee of the Society of Illustrators. Both partners are also members of the Graphic Artists Guild, and Barbara is a regular contributing editor to both *Communication Arts Magazine* and *Freelancers' News*. In addition, she has written for *Photo District News*, *Art Direction* magazine, *Photo Design*, the *Photographer's Marketplace*, the *Photographer's Guide to Marketing and Self-Promotion*, *The Artist's Marketplace*, *Design Studio News*, and *American Artist Magazine*. Both of them are also desired speakers at professional organization meetings and art schools throughout the country.

In addition, Elliott Gordon is director of Pratt Institute's Associate Degree program in graphic design and illustration.

Barbara and Elliott, with their two sons and two cats of suspect heritage (the cats, not the boys), have homes in both New York and Connecticut.